The New American Millionaires

Praise for
The New American Millionaires

This is a MUST READ if you want to *really* learn how people built mega-successful businesses with no advantages. Dr. Ken Odiwe has managed to synthesize the mind of the business genius and has done so in a way that can be absorbed by any business leader—aspiring or otherwise—no matter their background. Dr. Odiwe interviews some of the most influential entrepreneurs of this millennium with incredible detail and reveals the secrets that launched each of them into the successful business stratosphere.

—Stefanie Hartman
Marketing & Entrepreneurial Expert
www.stefaniehartman.com

The New American Millionaires has plenty of answers. It offers more than its share of insights into what it takes to be a successful entrepreneur in this country. But more than that, it boasts something you just don't find in many books of the genre: inspiration. Upon reading Dr. Odiwe's story and learning the New American Millionaire model, I find myself completely inspired. And you will, too.

—Rick Frishman
Founder Planned Television Arts,
PR Maven, Publisher.

The New American Millionaires sheds light on a verifiable model for what it means—and more importantly, what it takes—to find success in business. The immigrant spirit is what made this country great. Today, that immigrant spirit has returned again to dominate the entrepreneurial landscape. No one has done a better or more thorough job of explaining *why*. But Dr. Odiwe takes it one step further, as well: he provides the *how*."

—Jill Lublin
International Speaker, Master Publicity Strategist, three-time Best Selling Author of *Guerilla Publicity*, *Networking Magic*, and *Get Noticed Get Referrals*.
www.PublicityCrashCourse.com/freegift

The face of the rich and powerful in America is changing. In this book, *The New American Millionaires*, Dr. Ken sheds light on not only why the United States is the greatest land of opportunity for those willing to work hard, but also on how a new breed of immigrants are becoming the business leaders and influence-makers of tomorrow. Supported by advice from some of today's top immigrant wunderkinds and his own rags to riches story, he offers entrepreneurs a recipe to chart their own courses to prosperity. Read every word of this book. You'll be glad you did.

—Mike Litman
#1 best-selling author of
Conversations with Millionaires

Damn! This is one of the books I wish I had put out there. As an immigrant myself, I've always been fascinated by the notion that there's something different about why immigrants seem to succeed more. Ken really opens up some good insight on this for others to follow their path.

—Yanik Silver
author of *Maverick Startup*

As you follow the journey of these *New American Millionaires* who have all trodden the same path you plan to venture down, you'll draw inspiration and hope, strength and confidence, knowledge and wisdom, from their travails and triumphs. This is much more than a "business book" or a "success manual." It's an inspirational guide, a self-development workbook, and a motivational wake-up call, all rolled into a simple, easy, and enjoyable read. Dr.Ken's treatise places us on the shoulders of the giants of our times. Read his book. Take heart from what you see. And live your dreams.

—Dr.Mani Sivasubramanian
Heart Surgeon, Infopreneur, and Social Entrepreneur

Millionaire-maker books are a dime a dozen, but every once in a while, a brilliant author will release a book that actually has the potential to change people's lives. This is one of those books.

— J.J. Childers
Author of *Real Wealth Without Risk* and *Asset Protection 101*

Whether you're an aspiring entrepreneur, a struggling small business owner, or a business leader looking to improve your game, you will find valuable solutions in this book. Dr. Ken's story is truly inspiring, and the insights he shares from some of the most successful entrepreneurs working today might just change your life.

—Bernadette Boas
Coach, Author, Speaker, Radio Personality,
and creator of the movement Shedding the Bitch®

Every once in a very, very long while, I come upon a book that makes me stop and take note…Imagine my pleasant surprise as I started reading *The New American Millionaires*, by Dr. Ken Odiwé. I discovered that it does not matter whether one defines success in terms of money, peace, or just happiness; [Dr. Ken's] secrets will help almost anyone to achieve success in life. I could go on and on expounding on the wonders of this marvelous volume, but I do not want to deprive the reader of the thrill of discovery or the joy of remembering the simple secrets of success. Read this book and re-read it as often as possible. It will re-awaken in you the memory of the infinite possibilities that reside within your heart and soul. It will serve as a guide to that which you are seeking.

—John Harricharan
Award-winning author of the bestseller,
When You Can Walk on Water, Take the Boat

Why can't YOU be rich? Others have come to America penniless, unable to speak English, and with no safety net, yet have become millionaires anyway! You'll love what Dr. Ken has gleaned from some of today's brightest minds who started with nothing on their way to success, but let nothing stop them either! Read this book today.

—Martin Wales
www.MartinWales.com

The single greatest challenge for any entrepreneur is to take that first step—to overcome that fear of failure and begin making their dreams a reality. Finally, someone has stepped forward to provide solutions for conquering that common fear. For anyone who yearns to start or owns a mega-successful business, *The New American Millionaires* is a must-read.

—C. Nwachukwu Okeke
Ph.D. Author of Law Books and Acclaimed Professor
of International and Comparative Law, Golden Gate
University of School of Law, San Francisco California.

The mark of any great how-to author is simply this: authenticity. Given that Dr. Ken has lived the immigrant story he so compellingly shares, you will be hard pressed to find a more authentic source. Dr. Odiwe knows that his model for success works because he has *lived it* himself.

—Alicia Lyttle
CEO Monetized Marketing, LLC
www.alicialyttle.com

Very rarely does one encounter a book on entrepreneurship that offers this much real and useful information. With his New American Millionaire model, Dr. Ken Odiwe provides an absolute game-changer for anyone who aspires to achieve greatness in a startup or existing business venture.

—John Paul Carinci
Author of *An All-Consuming Desire To Succeed*

The New American Millionaires challenges those who dream of success to take their outlook to a new level. Those who follow Dr. Ken's model will immediately gain the kind of resourcefulness and innovation it takes to become a true leader in business.

—Frank Garon
Internet Guru and Real Estate Mastermind

If you are adventurous and keen on climbing the rather treacherous ladder of business success, you must read every word of this book. It will give you the confidence of champions.

—Dr. Joe Vitale,
Author of *Attract Money Now,* www.AttractMoneyNow.com

The time for this book is NOW! These are challenging economic times. Dr. Ken's book will bring many entrepreneurs out of the pangs of economic woes and help them to build highly competitive businesses.

—Jason Oman
TV Success Story
#1 Best-Selling author of *Conversations with Millionaires*,
Conversations with Female Millionaires, & *Millionaire Money Formula*

The New American Millionaires

*Secrets the Self-Made Millionaires Use
to Achieve Massive Levels of Success*

Dr. Ken Odiwé

NEW YORK

The New American Millionaires
Secrets the Self-Made Millionaires Use to Achieve Massive Levels of Success

ISBN 978-1-61448-386-1 paperback
ISBN 978-1-61448-387-8 eBook
Library of Congress Control Number: 2012951256

Morgan James Publishing
The Entrepreneurial Publisher
5 Penn Plaza, 23rd Floor,
New York City, New York 10001
(212) 655-5470 office • (516) 908-4496 fax
www.MorganJamesPublishing.com

Cover Design by:
Brenda Haun
BHaundesigns@gmail.com

Interior Design by:
Bonnie Bushman
bonnie@caboodlegraphics.com

In an effort to support local communities, raise awareness and funds, Morgan James Publishing donates a percentage of all book sales for the life of each book to Habitat for Humanity Peninsula and Greater Williamsburg.

Get involved today, visit
www.MorganJamesBuilds.com.

DEDICATED to the memory of my father, Chief Gabriel Obi Odiwé, whose inspiration to achieve has been the guiding light of my life.

Dad instilled the importance of discipline, focus, perseverance, courage and humility—all characteristics of the "torch of life" he passed down to me.

Table of Contents

Foreword

I WAS HONORED WHEN Dr. Ken Odiwe approached me to ask if I would be willing to contribute to his book. It never occurred to me that, despite my childhood experiences with my Chilean family, neighbors, and teachers, I had developed some of the same traits Dr. Ken outlines in the pages to come. Upon reading the book, it became quite clear to me that he had tapped into something incredible—he had found a link between the immigrant spirit and a series of powerful tools designed to create wealth.

There's something so powerful about landing in a foreign country and trying to make your own way. One must adapt to different people, food, values, and customs—indeed a completely different way of *being*. It's a tough situation, but as my family taught me, it is one that can only make you stronger.

I remember from my childhood many scenes of my parents meeting with family friends every weekend. Together, the adults would plan their futures, both individually and collectively. Most were in dire straits, working in what we considered "menial jobs," and yet they all had a vision: one day, they would overcome their difficult financial circumstances by moving to America, the most prosperous country in the world. Over the course of many weekends scattered across several years, they would devise a plan that would put them on the path to the American Dream.

As a young girl of twelve (and through the age of fifteen) sitting in on these meetings, little did I know that I was learning many of the timeless principles of success covered in this book. Naïve as I was, I listened in on the conversations. I witnessed the enthusiasm, the hope, and the dreams of these amazing men and women. All of them were keen to become millionaires—they would be, after all, working in the ultimate land of opportunity.

The men would play poker on Saturday nights. The families would gather for barbeques on the beach. We all celebrated birthdays and holidays together. But through it all, the question of how to surpass their circumstances was always foremost in the conversation. When the dream finally began to take hold as a plan of action, the families pooled their money together and began embarking upon a series of entrepreneurial projects. They were intent on success. In their minds, low-paying jobs and the potential for poverty simply was not an option. This refusal to accept the hands they were dealt is something that has stuck with me even today.

At the Excellerated Business School®, we teach our participants to constantly ask themselves the following questions:

"How can I leverage myself today?"

"How can I leverage my products/services?"

"How can I continue to expand my network/market for my business?"

In their own way, my immigrant role models were asking the same empowering questions every day. And in my own way, I grew up surrounded by these questions, which in turn led to my determination and drive to achieve.

Success doesn't happen by accident. There is a formula. There are distinctions and principles that must be present in order to make it so. With this book, you will learn those distinctions and principles—and you will do so in a way that is easy to absorb, process, and adapt to your life. Even from Page 1, it is clear that Dr. Ken has put tremendous energy and effort into offering a concise and precise piece of work. The result of this organization and research will lead to true and measurable results for you.

The subject of how to attain wealth seems a universal question in the minds of people residing in civilized countries. In many ways, it's the "holy grail" of the 21st Century. Once one realizes that this wealth is at our fingertips—that it can be reached by any reasonable human being that is open to new ideas, is willing to learn from the masters, and who doesn't allow for old-thinking to come into play—it becomes little more than a matter of sweat and tears. Achieving wealth is possible. It can be done. By *anyone*.

With this book, Dr. Ken shares these same lessons with you, along with a host of new business principles that will help you to create the wealth about which you have always dreamed. Congratulations! You have stumbled into some good stuff here. Read Dr. Ken's principles, test his strategies, put the New American Millionaire model to work. These are powerful, proven tools for success. I wish you all the productivity and prosperity that they promise.

—Dame DC Cordova
CEO Excellerated Business School®
for Entrepreneurs / Money & You®

Introduction

Out With the Old Rules

IS THIS THE TIME to turn your life around? In answering this age-old question, I ask that you merely take a look around you. What do you see? I see economic turmoil. In recent years the American dream has taken a considerable hit. The rug has been pulled out by a collapsing real estate market, a stagnating jobs outlook, and tumultuous performances on the stock exchanges. The gap between rich and poor has widened. The government often stalls on even the most inconsequential issues. Millions of protestors have turned out all across the country to "occupy" the financial system. Perhaps more than ever before, the United States isn't the sole driver of the global economy. Where it used to dictate the terms of international economic conditions based on its own consumer demand and gross domestic product, it is now very much at the mercy of the expansion and contraction of other world economies. Countries all over the globe suffer from debt crises. The dollar is weakening. In the eyes of some economists, the entire system is in danger of collapse.

These are strange and frightening times. Certainly this is no time to follow the old rules. Where the generations that came before us were often able to get by and even generate a little wealth for themselves on the back of hard labor and decent jobs, millions of Americans now struggle just to pay their bills. Major corporations lay off workers by the thousands. Others employ their workers at salaries far lower than might have seemed reasonable as recently as ten years ago. More and more, people must take on second and even third jobs just to make ends meet.

Clearly the path to wealth and the American dream has shifted. This country enjoyed a brief period of promise for all who worked hard; that promise now seems to be reserved solely for those companies already established or those companies fortunate enough to be in the right place at the right time to develop and sell the next big thing.

The times have changed dramatically for entrepreneurs as well. In this frightening new world, fewer and fewer people make it as small business owners. Established corporations are so giant and so firmly rooted it's often extraordinarily difficult to carve out even a small slice of market share. With the government landscape in the US uncertain and the economic picture unstable, there is simply no security for the entrepreneur. What used to be a risky proposition is now an overwhelming challenge. The only security in this unsecure environment is one's own effort and initiative.

At the same time, the playing field is changing. More than ever before, the men and women responsible for the largest companies on the planet hail from countries outside the United States. For every Warren Buffet, there is a Sergey Brin, the Russian-born cofounder of Google, and a Vinod Khosla, the Indian cofounder of Sun Microsystems. For every Bill Gates, there is an Andrew Grove, the Hungarian cofounder of Intel, and Elon Musk, the South African/Canadian cofounder of PayPal. I call people like these the New American Millionaires—people who have come to this country and used their inherent immigrant spirit to embark upon wildly successful entrepreneurial endeavors, first-generation Americans who have come to lead some of the most powerful, influential, and profitable companies in the world.

Even a cursory glance across the expanse of American business will demonstrate that the marketplace has become substantially more global. Gone are the days when an entrepreneur had to compete merely with the businesses down the street. Those days have been undercut by the Internet and the globalized economy. We have moved from a time when America was the singular land of opportunity to a time when America is merely the staging ground.

So with all that in mind, it seems safe to say change is in the air. The way we used to think about what makes a successful business no longer applies. The playing field is different and the players are more diverse in background. Businesses must be more innovative and more willing to adapt than ever before. Startups can become mega-corporations almost overnight (and then move into bankruptcy nearly as quickly). The landscape of the current market could not be more different from the landscape we saw prior to the tech boom of the '90s. We must throw the old rules *and* the new rules about how to become financially successful out the window.

Fortunately there's good news. For all the changes we have seen in the economy and the marketplace, we can observe few changes in the traits that make a millionaire a millionaire to begin with. The mental, social, and professional makeup of today's millionaire is hardly different from that of the millionaire of the 1980s, the 1950s, the 1930s, or even the 1800s—at least not when it comes to the qualities that make him particularly apt to becoming a successful businessperson.

The millionaire of today has simply adapted to the new world order. It seems logical, then, to say if we hope to learn how to become millionaires we must not study some elusive and ever-changing *method* of achieving riches—as almost every mega-millions book on the shelf attempts to do—but rather we must study the *people* who walked that path. In much the same way that Napoleon Hill attempted to define the millionaire of the 1930s, we must attempt to define the millionaire of today. Only then will we learn how to think and grow rich in this modern market.

To meet that end, we must first ask what we know about the millionaire of today. I have already hinted at the answer. Increasingly the millionaire of today is someone who was born in a country other than the United States. This is not to suggest the US hasn't produced its fair share of remarkable innovators in recent years. It certainly has.

What I mean to point out is that in an increasingly globalized market, trends suggest an increasingly diverse pool of thinkers and innovators is rising to the top. Not since the start of the Industrial Revolution has such a high percentage of American businesses been founded or run by people born outside the US. I believe steadfastly that the qualities and strategies of these New American Millionaires represent the proverbial key to becoming rich in this country.

Now, before I go even one sentence further with this line of thinking, please allow me to offer a very important point: This book is not just for recent immigrants to the US. This book is for everyone. Why? Because the traits that make New Americans so apt to generate riches can be *learned*. And if they can be learned, they can be adopted and implemented in the lives of literally any entrepreneur regardless of background. The traits I intend to outline in this book are universal. They are the very lifeblood of what makes a person successful in this country. Armed with the knowledge of exactly what makes an American entrepreneur rich—and, of course, through a little hard work and tireless effort—you too can use the lessons of the New American Millionaires and amass riches beyond your wildest dreams.

Additionally I should draw your attention to the fact that nearly everyone born in this country finds his familial roots somewhere beyond its shores. The United States is a nation of immigrants. The people most responsible for shaping this country and making it what it is today (in the governmental, entrepreneurial, and social sense) were born in countries other than the United States. The founding fathers of the United States were all first-generation Americans, taught and influenced by immigrants from other countries. Stephen Girard, John Jacob Astor, Andrew Carnegie, and dozens of other champions of American banking and industry were born outside the US.

Even if you identify yourself as solely American, odds are good that your grandparents or great-grandparents were born in a foreign land. The short of it is that we are all immigrants in some ways. Immigrants founded this country, they made this country great, and they have led directly to the diverse and highly entrepreneurial population that exists today. They have contributed so much to the success of this nation simply because they have long lived by a formula for generating wealth and building successful businesses.

A cursory glance across today's ultracompetitive and ever-changing business world suggests some things will never change. The immigrant spirit founded this country and made it great. In many ways that same immigrant spirit has contributed to the remarkable profits generated by some of America's most successful modern companies. When it came to wealth generation and company building, the New American Millionaire spirit worked for thousands of New Americans in the 1700s through the 1900s. Interestingly the New American Millionaire spirit appears to be working in much the same way today. There is something about being new to this country that allows a select few individuals to hold the key to considerable wealth. Perhaps if we could learn how to identify and use this key for ourselves then literally anyone, regardless of background, could open the path to unstoppable riches.

So what is the key? It lies in the personal traits and professional factors that make these New American Millionaires capable of generating so much wealth in the United States. Remarkably my research has shown a direct correlation between these factors and the traits and belief structures that allowed these New Americans to leave their homelands behind in favor of new lives in the United States. In other words the things that made them capable of becoming millionaires are the same things that made them willing and able to immigrate. So if we can identify where the drive to immigrate to the US meets the drive to generate wealth through entrepreneurship—if we can learn to think not just like a millionaire but like a New American Millionaire, we can begin to understand exactly *how* to achieve riches.

In this book I intend to speak on the topic of wealth generation in the New American Millionaire way not simply as a researcher but as a man who has walked the same path. Much like the high-profile New American Millionaires I interviewed for this book, I was born outside this country. In similar fashion, for the first several years I spent on these shores, I struggled mightily with finances and sometimes with just fitting in to the culture. Like the New American Millionaires I followed a path to success in this country that was born of the values intrinsic to my upbringing. These traits are exactly what have made so many New Americans rich. And they can make you rich too, no matter where you were born.

In addition my path to riches caused me to meet and learn from a large number of millionaires. My studies have led me to a unique understanding of what it takes to generate wealth. I have spent many hours, weeks, months, and years piecing together everything that separates the one percent of wealthy Americans from the other ninety-nine percent.

Finally I have conducted literally hundreds of hours of interviews with some of the world's most influential New American Millionaires. Their lessons have fueled the creation of my model for riches, reinforcing the principles I intend to share in the pages to come. In addition to these insights, I will share with you passages from the interviews themselves. You will gain direct access to the minds of the very people who are shaping the new global economy. In many ways this book is an exposé of their thoughts. From the minds of the New American Millionaire to yours, you will learn the secrets of success.

I recognize there is a veritable sea of books on entrepreneurship and wealth generation. Given that, you might ask what separates this book from all the others. It is a fair question, and one with a simple answer: unlike the other books on how to become rich, this one provides an extensively tested model that demonstrates not just anecdotal or small sample success rates but rather a model with a centuries-old track record of success. Further, unlike other books that often hint at the fringes of what makes a millionaire a millionaire—books designed solely to get you to buy the accompanying DVD or attend the essential seminar—I will offer my model with elegant simplicity and rich detail. By the time you are finished reading these pages you will have gained tremendous insight into not just how a broad range of New Americans have become rich but *why* as well. In knowing the *why*, your journey toward unstoppable riches begins.

Perhaps your dream is to quit your nine–to-five job so you may start your own business. Maybe you've lost your job and are looking for new ways to make a living in this uncertain market. Or maybe your dream to start your own business has already been realized. In all cases this book will provide the answers for how to take your dream to the next level. Read on to discover how you can become a better fundraiser and fund manager, securing the kind of capital it takes to turn a fledgling company into a growing company. Read on for the secrets for turning fear into fearlessness, allowing you the strength and poise to take the risks necessary to achieving success. Read on to learn how to think like an outsider, using your unique mindset to leverage an advantage over the competition. Read on to see how a burning desire (for success, for growth, and for profit) can lead to an upward trajectory for your company unlike anything you have previous imagined.

Read on as well for tips on how to enhance your spirit of adventure, opening up doors that might have otherwise been closed. Read on for ways to innovate beyond anything you thought possible, unleashing your potential to meet established market needs (or even create the next big thing). Read on to learn how to find resources where you thought you only had deficits, enhancing your resourcefulness to the point of turning dire situations into advantages. Read on to assume a new level of creative and professional drive, one that will propel you to new heights. Read on to harness your competitive spirit, allowing you to better yourself and those around you. And read on for the secrets of how to delegate tasks to people you can count on to make yourself capable of doing the work of twelve people instead of one.

Our journey to this knowledge begins with an examination of what, specifically, drives the New American Millionaire toward riches. In each chapter the journey begins with a portion of my life story, an illustration of how my decision to come to this country and suffer through my many initial struggles eventually put me on the path to the success I enjoy today. These excerpts will be followed by the stories and anecdotes provided by the many New American Millionaires interviewed for this book. Each chapter then provides tips and strategies for how to absorb a specific New American Millionaire quality into your life—the kind of qualities that will put you on the path to financial gain. You will learn the traits that allowed each New American Millionaire to travel to this country, begin generating wealth, and then put that wealth to work creating wildly successful businesses. Through explanation of these traits I will establish a model that, with a little hard work and dedication, can be emulated. Once you have learned these lessons, I will demonstrate exactly how to make them work for you.

So do not fret over the dangers of the current economy. Yes, the business environment is cloudier than it has been in quite some time. But the beauty of the New American Millionaires model is that it works in both good times and bad. It works for established entrepreneurs as well as aspiring ones. It works for those with capital to burn and for those with empty pockets. If you only take the time to learn these lessons and make them a part of your business life you will be well on your way to reaching the next level of success in your entrepreneurial endeavors.

So let's return to our original question: is this the time to turn your life around? It is an excellent question, one that each of us must ask at some point in our lives—particularly whenever we are faced with challenging economic circumstances like those we endure at the time of this writing. But a more direct question given these circumstances is: are you ready to receive the secrets that have catapulted a remarkable number of people toward stupendous riches in America?

If your answer to this question is "yes," then you must read every word of this book. In fact do not just read them; devour them. Incorporate their lessons. Visit **www.milliondollarsuccessinstitute.com** for a set of free high-powered tools that will help you make the coming lessons a part of your life. Then get down to the business of generating tremendous wealth for yourself—the business of becoming a New American Millionaire.

Chapter 1

The Night the Metallic Bird Flew

My First Step Toward Becoming a New American Millionaire

We have performed the act of which all men anciently dream, the thing for which they envy the birds; that is to say, we have flown.
—Salman Rushdie1

WELCOME TO AMERICA. These are the words every New American has longed to hear at one point or another in his or her life. To you I say, "Welcome to the *new* America." And welcome to the secrets of the New American Millionaires. In the pages to come, I will present in no uncertain terms my findings based on nearly a decade of research— findings that demonstrate a quantifiable and learnable model for achieving riches in the United States.

Here you will find the secrets of dozens of successful entrepreneurs who have brazenly flown away from their own cultures and into John

---

1   Rushdie, S. (1984). *Shame*. New York: Aventura/Vintage.

F. Kennedy International Airport, each of them leaving behind family, friends, and everything they have ever known so they could set out in search of their dreams. To know their secrets is to know how to become rich. You will read their stories. You will learn about the paths of some of the wealthiest New American Millionaires, from their earliest struggles to their latest successes. You will see exactly how they have climbed from the depths of poverty to the heights of fulfilled lives and unimaginable riches. You will learn how to think like a New American Millionaire.

If we examine enough data and mine enough information from the vast histories of successful entrepreneurship, we find New Americans are particularly well equipped to achieve riches in America. Even a quick look at the founders or current CEOs of the most successful corporations in this country suggests New Americans have established a demonstrated pathway to success that borrows from a specific manner of thinking about work, education, entrepreneurship, relationships, marriage, raising children, and, above all, seizing opportunity in America. When you have read these pages, you will find as I have found: that immigrant entrepreneurs seem to possess something inherent to their natures; they are more apt to be big dreamers and more willing to work hard to achieve.

All entrepreneurs, regardless of their cultural backgrounds, can gain from the lessons provided in this book. The reason for this is simple: the New American Millionaires I studied were not born with all the qualities it takes to find success in the United States. On the contrary they are typical in many aspects of their lives. Most came from humble family backgrounds, thriving under meager means of existence. But there are common threads woven into the very fabric of these men and women, and studying these threads will benefit you greatly.

For one, each New American Millionaire has *flown* from their homelands to America, faced myriad challenges, and, in the end, made it big in this melting pot of milk and honey. It is perhaps in this very act of flying that New American entrepreneurial success finds its roots. Migration from one's country of birth to another in search of the proverbial greener pastures is in itself an act of entrepreneurship.

Being an entrepreneur involves a higher propensity for risk, after all, and what greater risk is there than leaving behind everything you've ever known?

An individual who chooses to emigrate consciously abandons a known environment, culture, social relations, and possibly the ability to be understood in his or her birth language. In return he is provided no assurances, only possibilities. An individual who makes such a choice demonstrates distinctive and possibly advantageous personality traits that may include a high tolerance for ambiguity, a propensity for risk taking, and a tendency to persevere through difficult times.

For most New Americans, the early days, weeks, and months following their arrival in the United States tend to be anxious and fraught with risk and uncertainty—a time of navigating between a foreign present and a lost past. Regardless of where the New Americans come from, in all cases the primary motivation for migration is the desire for better opportunities for development. But when they arrive, they find not a life of ease and luxury, as perhaps they had imagined, but a rude awakening—a culture shock so stirring it impacts their very identities as individuals. The shock often results in periods of stress, depression, frustration, fear, alienation, and pessimism. Given these same circumstances, most people would likely give up, return home, try something new. But in the cases of the New American Millionaires, *something* causes them to persevere.

As an entrepreneur much of your competition has strived since birth to make it in America. Many of them have worked hard all their lives simply to leave their home countries for this one. Wanting more than anything to succeed—to carve out their own paths here in support of their families—they fought tooth and nail to make their dreams realities. On the way they faced many daunting challenges. They saw financial trouble and social difficulty. But they had in their personalities everything it takes to overcome these obstacles and then some. They naturally knew what needed to be done to succeed.

Do you have that same drive? Can you look into the face of certain failure and ignore it? Can you innovate in ways that will make you rise above the competition? Can you do great things with few resources? And can you do all of this even as the competition evolves into an arena that's bigger and more global than ever before?

To be successful you will need to be frugal. To be successful you will need to be fearless. To be successful you will need to have burning desire. You will need a grand sense of adventure. You will need to be more resourceful than the competition. You will have to out-innovate everyone in the marketplace. You must be driven, competitive, and unafraid to ask for help. And you must never stop learning.

Since you have come this far, I can assume you are looking for a different but tested way to change your financial future. But one thing I cannot assume is who you are as a person. I can't know your level of motivation, your energy, your drive, or your desire to be rich. What I can assure you is, if you are willing to put in the work, the secrets revealed in this book will help you to lift all the stones that have hindered your success in the past. If you put in the time to learn how to think like a New American Millionaire, together we will pull back the proverbial curtain and expose the secrets that have propelled some of the world's greatest movers and shakers to the highest pinnacles of success.

The act of pulling back the curtain begins with the story of my own immigration to the United States. But before I begin, let me provide you with a brief primer. As is the case with almost every immigrant who comes to this great country, my struggles upon arrival were enormous. I endured a number of failed attempts to adjust to my new environment. I tried to adapt. I tried to fit in. I tried to make enough money to get by. And in most cases, I failed. But the important thing about my story is that, as is the case with literally every successful person in this country (immigrant or otherwise), I quickly and resiliently hunkered down. I never gave up. Like Thomas Edison it took me a great many attempts at different entrepreneurial endeavors before I finally found a light at the end of the tunnel.

The night of my departure from the country of my birth was a muggy one, the stifling, tropical heat particularly oppressive as my parents and I made our way toward the airport and the metallic bird that would carry me to my new life. It was September and I was eighteen years old, fresh out of high school. My parents had long wanted me to have a world-class education, so they had trained their eyes on America. They had heard of the great universities here, and though I was shy and a little timid I was not so subdued as to make the journey seem unreasonable. It helped, of course, that I had graduated at the top of my high school class.

As we approached the airport, I felt a lump forming in my throat. At 8:00 p.m., a mere three hours hence, I would catch a flight bound for New York. My final destination would be the University of Illinois, which would serve as my new home and school for at least the next four years. Until that moment, with our car heading toward the airport, I had felt nothing but jubilation at the thought of studying in America. But now, as the reality loomed over me, for the first time I wanted nothing more than to forgo the idea of leaving my home, my friends, and the life I had always known.

The process of passing through check-in and security proved blindingly quick—far too fast for my anxious heart's liking. I said a hasty goodbye to my parents, both of them so proud, and departed through the gate and toward my destiny. As I stepped aboard the plane, I felt like a parcel of mail sealed, stamped, and on its way for delivery to America.

Life on campus at the U of I proved different from everything I knew. I had learned ahead of time that the language here was English. But I quickly realized American English is clearly distinct from the Queen's English I spoke so fluently—so distinct, in fact, it might as well have been called "American."

The first year of my new life passed slowly as I painfully adjusted to my surroundings and struggled to fit in and make friends. I faced almost constant problems with transportation, ever-increasing stress, and crippling loneliness. The final blow came toward the end of my first year when a letter from my parents arrived, announcing they could no longer afford to provide for me financially. If I wanted to make ends meet, I would be on my own: my most dreaded fear realized.

And so my second year of college loomed over me, my pockets empty and my prospects looking bleak. I spent several days feeling sorry for myself. I considered many times simply returning home. But then it occurred to me, as it must occur to most immigrants who face similar situations: I simply *couldn't* go home. That would be a disgrace to myself and my family. Come what may I had to make my life work in my new home country.

So I pulled myself together. I picked up the pieces. And I formulated a plan. I found there was no way I could pay for my school fees and lodging with the meager jobs I could gain in Illinois. Also I was far lonelier than I ever could have imagined prior to leaving my home country. Fortunately I had an aunt who lived in San Francisco. Upon my inquiry she invited me to come join her there, where I could enter the University of California system, take on odd jobs, and live with her. Considering my dwindling prospects in Illinois, this suited me nicely.

In this way my second year of college began in California. At the start of the first semester, I was going to school full-time and working part-time. My jobs were lowly. I did everything from cleaning toilets on campus to driving a shuttle bus for other students. Even so it was difficult for me to make tuition each semester. I would have to get promissory notes from the university that would allow me to take classes and then pay for them at semester's end. If I failed to pay, the university would simply cancel my attendance and record from the semester as if I had never attended at all. I often found myself scraping to get by, and on more than one occasion I missed the cutoff date for paying for a previous semester.

When my aunt moved out of the area to pursue a new career, I would turn to taking a new apartment on my own. I moved from apartment to apartment for a time because I would inevitably get behind on rent and wind up evicted. It got to the point where I had to start living in my car. Meals were scarce. I would occasionally go to a friend's house for dinner. On these occasions I would ask permission to use the shower, saying I had forgotten to shower at home and would need to clean up before going to work. Afterward I would return to my car to sleep.

I went back and forth like this for two years. It was a level of poverty and desperation I had never known at home. Indeed every month that passed seemed to make home look more and more attractive. But I knew I could never go back to where I had started. That bridge was burned. I simply couldn't return home. It was (and is) so entrenched in my mind, culture, and spirit that once you are given the opportunity to carve a new path in America, you cannot forsake that opportunity. You simply have to dig out and do whatever it takes to succeed.

My path to success first presented itself during my junior year. I had the good fortune of meeting an immigrant businessman who had found his niche in the business world. For our purposes I will call this man Amos. He must have noticed the desperation in my eyes, because he immediately began talking to me about his own struggles upon first immigrating to America. As he told his story, though, it became clear these struggles were very much in the past. Amos was now a man of insurance and real estate. He had not yet made his first million at the time, but it seemed evident that he was well on his way. The plan for his future had been cemented in his mind, and he knew his path to riches and to success. He was even willing to share that path with me. I only had to listen to his advice.

With few other options, I left school and began working with Amos in financial sales. Perhaps it was a natural drive for selling or perhaps it was because I absorbed so much of what my new friend taught me, but I enjoyed great success in the business almost immediately. Within my first year, I had done a million dollars of business for my company. This was the beginning of my turnaround. In relatively short order, I had gone from scrubbing toilets to making a quarter of a million dollars of personal income in one year. It was enough money for me to begin dabbling in school again. I reenrolled at the university, earned my undergraduate degree, and began working toward an advanced degree.

When I'd earned my degrees, I found it was easier to work in financial sales. My education opened new doors. I was able to sell bigger-ticket plans to corporations rather than smaller plans to individuals. This exposure taught me how to sell to and deal with corporate leaders. I used this new knowledge to propel me on a foray into the real estate market. I began buying houses and acquiring assets. By my thirty-third birthday, I was worth more than a million dollars.

I do not write these things to brag. I wish only to demonstrate that my determination led me down a path many others have followed. As you will see, I am certainly not the first and only immigrant with a story like this to tell. So many others have experienced these same things. In fact it was that very thought that led me to research the subject. When I looked at my ledger and realized I was a thirty-three-year-old millionaire, I began to think, *If this could happen to me, why doesn't it happen to everyone?* Not just immigrants but *everyone?* It seemed to me that *anyone* with the proper family values, work ethic, drive, and determination could succeed as Amos and I had. We got to where we were (and are) because we refused to let anything stop us. We never viewed our immigrant statuses as detrimental. And we always aspired to bigger and more fulfilling careers.

It seemed to me I was on to something. I felt like I had stumbled onto a pattern that could be made into a science—a true and measurable model that could be taught to other people with similar drive and motivation. What if there were a way to quantify the things that had made me so successful? And, better yet, what if there were a clear way to relate those things to other people?

This idea was all well and good. But I was a man of learning now. I wasn't satisfied with the idea of the New American Millionaire mindset as a science until I enrolled in a terminal degree program and began studying it thoroughly. I returned to university with the goal of earning my doctorate degree in pursuit of this science. I would use my research to build something that would help individuals and corporations succeed. It became my lifelong passion. I entered into a seven-year period of trying to confirm what I had lived and what I had observed in other immigrants like Amos and me. I identified the observable qualities of the New American Millionaire. Then I began testing to see whether the qualities truly led to success across the board. As I tested I began to coach other people on my findings. These people would come back with wonderful results. It seemed as if my research had been confirmed.

From that day until the day of this writing, I have been interviewing other New American Millionaires to confirm further whether Amos and I were flukes. As I close this chapter, I am happy to report we are not. After well over a decade of real-life experience and research, I feel comfortable concluding that this study is a viable science. I have discovered the model for true success in America. And the best part is this model can be taught to others.

If you wish to be one of these others, read on.

Chapter 2

What Motivates the New American Millionaire?

It All Starts with Your "Reason Why"

Success doesn't come to you; you go to it.
—Marva Collins

ALLOW ME TO BEGIN by telling you something you may already know: millionaires are not like other people. They do not possess the same personal, emotional, and mental makeup as the masses. There is something different, something more profound that drives them. Interestingly my years of research have demonstrated to me that these same qualities are what drive immigrants to travel to the US and establish themselves as New Americans as well. These qualities, taken together, represent a framework for success in business—a framework that has proven itself time and again in the sphere of entrepreneurship.

10

This chapter presents that framework and establishes the roots of how to make it a part of your life.

Before I go any further, let me make it clear that I am not suggesting a biological advantage here. Despite the fact that my book's title implies New American entrepreneurs are particularly adept at becoming millionaires, I am not suggesting these particular entrepreneurs hold some kind of evolutionary edge. The old yarn "millionaires aren't born, they're made" is entirely true. Sergey Brin's genetic makeup did not make him particularly apt to cofound one of the world's most successful mega-corporations; his upbringing and social stressors led to a number of personal traits that we may also observe in a significantly high percentage of other millionaires.

The reason Mr. Brin's immigrant status is of particular interest here is because many of the traits that led him to such staggering financial success are the very same traits that led him to make the leap from Russia to the United States in the first place. If not for the motivating factors that sparked him to leave family, friends, and the comfort of his birth language and country behind, he might not have had what it took to cofound Google. Without these factors he might still be living in the city of his birth, perhaps working for a salary as a midlevel programmer for some well-established Russian software company. And who knows whether we would have Google then?

Though they are born essentially the same as the rest of us, something changes for your average millionaires as they grow up. Often long before they even reach the age where they are championing fledgling companies, it is clear millionaires simply aren't like other people. If you're rich, you are by nature what we call *extraordinary*. Put simply, when compared to the average person, millionaires operate on an entirely different level of motivation.

The bad news is not everyone has what it takes to achieve this level of motivation. The good news is the things that motivate the millionaire can be learned. Be sure to visit **www.milliondollarsuccessinstitute. com** for deeper insight into the New American millionaire profile. But for now let's begin the learning process.

The Eleven Motivational Traits of the New American millionaire
We begin our examination of the millionaire mind by looking at some of the qualities I discovered millionaires share with many New Americans. These qualities are of particular value to us because they get to the root of what drives so many entrepreneurs to success. If you can learn and implement these qualities in your life, you will be well on your way to achieving your financial and personal dreams.

- **Trait #1:** New Americans and millionaire entrepreneurs are astute—they know how to spend, how to save, and how to borrow.

  Recent economic troubles suggest many people born into the United States have no idea how to save money. When the bubble burst in 2008, nine-to-fivers and entrepreneurs alike found themselves too in debt to survive economic despair. Much of modern American business is run on debt. Companies that are too leveraged are often the first to go during a downturn. They are also easily overpowered by their wiser-saving counterparts.

  Take this in juxtaposition to the New American. In many cases he comes to this country having already adopted wise spending and saving habits. Without these habits he might never have been able to raise the kind of money it takes to travel abroad and make his way in a new and demanding land. Once in the US, the New American is often saddled with more expenses than ever before. And, in many cases, he must meet these expenses while getting paid very little. The job prospects for a person working on a visa are few, after all. So too is the opportunity for credit. Where the average American can simply fill out an application and expect to be sent a credit card, the New American must pay for everything with the cash he earns.

  For these reasons the New American learns early that he must pay himself first. He realizes that without the ability to save aggressively he will never improve his lot in life. He will continue to struggle to make ends meet, and in the end he is likely to fail at his dream to survive in America.

The same truths can be extended to a successful entrepreneur. Some (but not many) have succeeded despite having to leverage a great deal of debt. These lucky few required more than a few positive breaks. More often than not, successful entrepreneurs—those who have achieved millionaire status—got to where they are because they learned how to use the financial resources they had at hand. They maximized their funds, and where those funds fell short they learned how to survive on other people's money (OPM). While the failing entrepreneur turned to his company credit card, the successful entrepreneur sought out investors to help him get by without accruing debt.

It's difficult to become a better manager of company funds. Fortunately, learning the habits of the money-wise is an entirely achievable venture. Do this and you will find that where others complain of never having enough, the money at your disposal will rarely be in short supply.

- **Trait #2:** New Americans and entrepreneurs are fearless—they do not shy away from daunting challenges.

Everyone is born into different circumstances, but we all have something in common: we learn to adapt to and live with those circumstances as we grow older. In some cases our circumstances are perfectly acceptable to us. Often, when this is the case, we grow into complacent and easily satisfied people. Others, however, are born into more trying circumstances. For these unlucky people, there are two paths: either they fold under the pressures of their living conditions or they do whatever it takes to improve them.

The latter require a remarkable kind of bravery. Imagine leaving behind everything you've ever known—your family, your friends, your home, your language, your culture. You must abandon everything that has ever meant something to you. For some the thought can be terrifying. These people often do not emigrate from their homelands. They remain in the situations that have troubled them since birth, always quick to discuss their dreams of leaving but never actually setting in motion the things they will need to achieve those dreams.

For others fear is not a consideration. These brave souls understand there is great risk to leaving behind everything and everyone they know. They understand coming to America means they will have to work hard—often harder than they have ever worked—just to establish themselves in their new home country. In many cases the American labor market will prevent them from obtaining the appropriate professional jobs for which they have been trained in their home countries (for example a lawyer in Portugal might find himself starting out as a taxi driver in the US). These New Americans realize they will have to make both personal and emotional sacrifices. They recognize their financial situation (at least in the short-term) is likely to be dire. And still they make the leap.

The same can be said for literally every successful entrepreneur operating in the United States. These people were intelligent and talented enough to take the safe jobs with midlevel salaries. But they all wanted something more. And unlike the people who settle for safes job with midlevel salaries, they were not afraid to fail. They knew there would be risks to pursuing their dreams, but they pursued them anyway. They understood they would have to face trying circumstances and challenges, and they did so with great determination.

- **Trait #3:** New Americans and entrepreneurs identify themselves as outsiders.

A person doesn't begin dreaming about living in another country unless he identifies himself as somehow different from those around him. New Americans are often more willing to take the leap to another country because they can already see themselves living there. They observe the people around them and realize that they somehow do not fit in—that their lives are meant for something more. Further they often view their peers as a kind of challenge. They tend to think the people around them don't believe they can make it in another country, so they set out to prove them wrong.

The same is often true of millionaires. Many millionaires suggest they have always felt as if their thinking processes differed from those of their peers. While most people go one way, they tend to go the other. They frequently identify a need to prove themselves to others—a kind of "me against the world" mentality that drives them constantly to do bigger and better things. They perceive their peers as somehow doubting them, and they dedicate their lives to proving them wrong.

This concept speaks to more than a motivation to disprove doubters, however. That "me against the world" mentality tends to lead a New American or entrepreneur to construct emotional walls that help him avoid getting hurt. Successful immigrants and entrepreneurs often hold on to a particular instance or series of instances from their lives where they were publicly degraded or humiliated. Whether it was a teacher chastising them in front of the class or friends mocking them for their dreams of traveling abroad, successful New Americans and entrepreneurs tend to take these experiences, embrace them, and make them a part of their identities. The emotional walls that result help them to make the kinds of decisions and perform the kinds of actions that others cannot—in business and in life.

• **Trait #4:** New Americans and entrepreneurs have a burning desire for success—they are more likely to be motivated by money, success, and other external reward factors.

Most people dream of being rich. Few achieve that dream. The only thing that separates the dreamers from the doers is motivation. The dreamers make little effort to improve their circumstances. In contrast the doers—the New Americans, the millionaires, and the New American Millionaire types—do whatever it takes to improve their circumstances.

New Americans find themselves attracted to a new country and in pursuit of personal, familial, social, financial, and/or political goals. They are often driven by less-than-ideal and, in some cases, oppressive conditions. Their home countries may be divided by social exclusion or discrimination or saddled with poor economies. They may find education and jobs are difficult to secure. Or they may find their religions or other belief systems are oppressed. Whatever the case the New American is someone who is unsatisfied with his current conditions and willing to do whatever needs to be done to improve them.

The same is true of the millionaire. While others dream of money and success, the millionaire goes out and gets them. Entrepreneurship is by its very nature the seeking of profit. A person is not likely to succeed in business or self-employment if one is not appropriately motivated to obtain profits—or at least to create a company that meets a perceived market need (and meets it well). Millionaires are the embodiment of that motivation.

- **Trait #5:** New Americans and entrepreneurs are adventurous—their spirit of adventure is what makes them so willing to take risks.

It takes a particular kind of bravery to go out into the unknown knowing full well nothing is promised to you. That bravery cannot be achieved without a spirit of adventure. If one is not willing to be the pioneer, the explorer, the founder, or the first to do something, one cannot be a millionaire. One must possess that can-do spirit if one hopes to find success in this country.

Most New Americans are no strangers to adventure. Traveling to and establishing themselves in the United States is itself an adventure. And so it is perhaps for this reason that so many New Americans are already equipped with the kinds of risk-taking personalities so common among successful entrepreneurs. New Americans are big dreamers, bold adventurers, and hard workers. These are three of the keys to finding success in a free market.

- **Trait #6:** New Americans and entrepreneurs are resourceful—where others struggle to find the money, help, or supplies needed to make something happen, successful New Americans and entrepreneurs always find ways to make the most of what they have.

  Not everyone is capable of saving the kind of money and lining up the kinds of opportunities it takes to leave one's home country in search of a new life. Some would-be New Americans fail to achieve their dreams simply because they are unwilling or unable to see and exploit the advantages available to them. Those who succeed do so because they have a keen understanding of the resources at their disposal—and, more importantly, the ability to exploit them, to use them to their advantage.

  This is also true of entrepreneurs. Far more entrepreneurs fail than succeed. Those who succeed do so because they are willing to use whatever resources and advantages they have before them. They are more apt than most to find ways to put everything at their disposal to good use.

  Where some New Americans' advantages lie in things like better access to education or parents with more money to spend on tickets abroad, entrepreneurs take advantage of things like access to information or niches that are closed off to other entrepreneurs. In either case the New American who successfully takes root in another country or the entrepreneur who becomes a millionaire does so because he is able to maximize his resources and exploit his advantages.

- **Trait #7:** New Americans and entrepreneurs are innovative—they possess the ability to perceive the needs of the marketplace and foresee the next big thing.

  As Jerry Yang, famed cofounder of Yahoo!, has noted, innovation is a matter of perceiving the needs of the marketplace. "We look at our users' interests," he said. "Without our users, we don't have business." A New American is someone who by nature seeks new opportunities. The same can be said of successful entrepreneurs, who, like New Americans, tend to be able to see a future that is preferable to the present. They are able to see concepts that will benefit themselves and those around them.

More importantly entrepreneurs are the kinds of people who are willing and able to make those concepts realities. Entrepreneurs are often motivated by an innate desire to create for the sake of creation—new products, services, works of art, work structures, living structures, etc. If there is a gap that can be filled by a new creation, entrepreneurs are always driven to fill it.

The true key is in the creation. Many people can dream. For every New American who dreams of coming to the United States, there are millions more would-be New Americans who dream the same thing. For every entrepreneur who creates a product or service that can change the future, there are millions more who had that same dream but did nothing to make it happen. The difference between the dreamers and the doers is the act.

- **Trait #8:** New Americans and entrepreneurs are focused and driven—they rarely allow external distractions to prevent them from achieving their goals.

  Successful New Americans and entrepreneurs are often more willing to do things that ordinary people aren't willing to do. Their drives are greater, as are their work ethics. They don't allow their emotions or even their health to get in the way of what needs to be done. A successful New American isn't going to pack up and move back home the moment he first faces adversity. Likewise a successful entrepreneur isn't going to stop trying to sell his idea because it's raining outside or he has a headache. People like these will instead move on, keep going, and continue doing what needs to be done.

  When the competition is busy making excuses or reorganizing their strategies, the successful entrepreneur is allowing his innovations, dreams, energy, and optimism to take over. Where others see obstacles, the successful entrepreneur sees opportunities. He finds the gaps in the marketplace and does everything he can—regardless of how many distractions might be swirling around him—to stay on task and fill them.

- **Trait #9:** New Americans and entrepreneurs are highly competitive—sometimes they are driven to beat the competition, but more importantly they are always driven to improve themselves.

  Whether winning means successfully establishing roots in a new country or championing a new and successful company, New Americans and entrepreneurs are uniquely driven to come out on top. And the desire to win goes deeper than that as well. It permeates everything in the lives of typical millionaires. It isn't simply an economic or social factor. The millionaire isn't driven solely by a desire to have more money than his neighbor. The New American isn't driven solely by a desire to live in a better country than his peers. No, people such as these never stop competing with themselves. No matter how much they achieve, they are never completely satisfied, and they always strive to better themselves.

- **Trait #10:** New Americans and entrepreneurs know how to delegate—where some people try to take on too much on their own, new Americans and entrepreneurs know how to maximize their efforts through the efforts of those around them.

  New Americans most often come to this country alone. Those who fail to make it here are typically the ones who feel too proud to ask for help. They figure that by leaning on others for support they are somehow cheapening their paths to success.

  But those who rise to greatness—those who come to establish companies that generate millions of dollars—do not get there alone. They learn early, as I did, that you simply *can't* do everything alone. Sometimes, to get ahead, you have to rely on the aid of others. You must accept handouts when they are offered. You must ask for help when it's needed. And you must learn to operate in business and in life with the efforts of those around you.

Successful entrepreneurs—particularly of the millionaire stock—often have excellent time-management skills. Where the average person might languish in all the work he has to get done, a successful entrepreneur knows how to delegate to others. He has a keen sense of how to get more hours out of his day. While others complain of not having enough time to complete their daily routines, millionaires are often churning out the work of several people for several days before they turn in and head home. They do this because they are willing and able to assign other people to the tasks for which they are responsible. And, more than that, they have learned to find the right people for the right tasks. They get more done because they are willing to lean on—and are extraordinarily adept at identifying opportunities for—other people's efforts (OPE).

- **Trait #11:** New Americans and entrepreneurs never stop learning—they understand an education does not necessarily begin or end at a formal university.

  The vast majority of the New Americans I interviewed for this book came to this country for one reason: the higher education system is second to none. Almost everyone I spoke to came to this country for the promise of a better education. And while this point is important, it is not the kind of education most cited by the millionaires I interviewed.

  There is an old cliché that we never stop going to school. This is true only of those people who are willing to keep their eyes open to—and, more importantly, learn from—the lessons of everyday life. The difference between a New American who succeeds in laying down roots in this country and a New American who must pack up and return home is often an ability to adapt. No matter what we do in life, we always have preconceived notions of what a particular undertaking will require. More often than not, that undertaking winds up requiring very different things than what we had previously imagined. Those who succeed in such undertakings are those most able to learn from their mistakes and adapt their approaches. These people then find themselves armed with a greater knowledge of what it takes to succeed in this country.

The same can be said of entrepreneurs. While it is true many successful entrepreneurs possess impressive degrees from high-level universities, it is also true that few of them will tell you the things they learned in the classroom are more important than the things they learned in the early days of establishing their businesses. No matter how much school we attend, nothing can compare to the hands-on nature of learning in the field. It is the best and often the only way to learn the intricacies of succeeding in the business world. Every business and every market is different, but with the lessons we can glean from New Americans and entrepreneurs alike, we can come to a better understanding of how to keep our education ongoing and how to make those things we learn work for us.

The Obstacles Before You

The idea of taking the eleven traits ingrained in the New American millionaire mindset and making them your own might seem overwhelming. For this reason your most substantial obstacle to success is the thought that you can't do it—that it's too difficult. You might also fear the notion that you don't have anyone available to coach you. You are without a mentor. You must do this alone.

Accepting these eleven traits as a part of your life will be a challenge. But it is a challenge that you are well-equipped to meet. You do not have to do it alone either. Visit my mastery web site: **www.MillionDollarSuccessInstitute.com** to be connected with hundreds of other entrepreneurs embarking upon the same journey. Here you will find all the tools you need to turn this incredible strategy into your reality as an entrepreneur.

If you absorb the knowledge in the pages to come—and, more importantly, do everything in your power to put that knowledge into action—you will find yourself achieving previously unimaginable success in this new marketplace. You can do this. These rules are rules for a reason: they have worked for centuries. What worked for Andrew Carnegie worked for Sergey Brin and will work for you. Take these secrets and these eleven traits to heart and watch your business grow. Then watch your riches grow right along with it.

The purpose of this chapter was to present you with an overview of the eleven specific traits that make an entrepreneur successful regardless of his or her background. If you can get to the point where these eleven traits can be used to describe you, then you will be well on your way to building a thriving business.

So you have your overview. Starting with the next chapter, you will gain exposure to the finer details that will help you make these traits a reality in your life. We will start off the New American Millionaire model with what is perhaps the most important aspect of business ownership: saving, spending, and managing money wisely. Read on to discover the secrets of how the best entrepreneurs earn, balance, and make the best use of their company finances.

Chapter 3

Astute: Smart Entrepreneurs Feather Their Nests

*Without frugality, none would be rich,
and with it very few would be poor.*
—Samuel Johnson

IF AMERICANS WERE NOT yet clear on whether their saving and spending habits were prudent, the economic recession that began in late 2008 removed all doubt. Thousands of small businesses—some of them possessing a marked level of success—went under as a result of the credit crunch. Too many entrepreneurs in this country were saving too little and leveraging far too much. Credit levels were at an all-time high. The imbalance between the average entrepreneur's debt and his ability to erase that debt became truly staggering.

Once inflationary pressures reached a boiling point, businesses began to have difficulty paying for the goods they relied upon each day. Banks, skittish about the teetering economy, simply were not lending the same cash to entrepreneurs that they had before. Businesses that relied heavily upon a consistent influx of cash had no choice but to close their doors. This led to jobs being cut in large swaths. Many Americans in the middle and lower classes were left with no incomes, higher costs of living, and overwhelming debt burdens. The outlook was bleak.

The lesson had been learned (at least by those who were willing to learn): if we hope to be financially responsible entrepreneurs—and, in the long run, financially successful—we need to become better at raising and saving liquid money. It's a simple enough lesson, but has it really taken effect?

It's strange how even the most ardent learners of the New American Millionaire way tend to overlook this most basic of dictums: if you don't save, you don't advance your financial outlook. You can't expect to become a millionaire if you don't maintain wise spending and saving habits. The millionaire isn't the man with the mortgage on his sprawling, suburban mansion, the loans on his three high-end cars, and the credit-card-purchased luxuries up to his eyeballs. That's a man with heavy debt. That's a man handcuffed to his financial present. That's a man who cannot afford an economic downturn.

Thinking like a New American Millionaire requires that we become more prudent, that we spend more time fluffing our nests and less time taking flight. Those who think in this way—those who find themselves on the path to unstoppable riches—are those with simple homes, modest cars, empty credit cards, and massive financial portfolios. They are financially solvent. They (and their businesses) own the things they keep. They are hardly at risk of financial collapse. They owe all of this to the fact that they rarely if ever purchased anything on credit. It is a simple concept—and a lesson as old as money itself—but they would never have become millionaires had they not made it the foundation of their financial lives.

New American Millionaires are more likely to follow wise spending and saving habits than the American-born. There is good reason for this: in order to come to America in the first place, the New American Millionaire and his family had to work and save hard to afford the journey. From a very early age, he practiced prudent saving strategies and pieced together the funds necessary to make his dreams realities. Just because he has now made it to American soil does not mean these long-ago ingrained strategies will disappear. He might be able to call himself an American now, but that does not mean he will begin spending like an American. Even if he wants to, he can't: because of his status, he is far less likely to be afforded credit to begin with. Working hard and saving are the only avenues for him to get ahead. Fortunately for him these avenues are tried and true—they are an unwavering path to riches. If you hope to emulate that path, you must learn to save like a New American Millionaire.

The Family Difference Makes the Difference

Spending and saving habits are often adopted from family circumstances. If a child is born into a family whose members buy whatever they want whenever they want, he is likely to grow up doing the same. If a child is born into a thrifty home, on the other hand, he is likely to count his pennies all his life. Fortunately, appropriate spending and saving habits don't have to be hard-wired. They are lessons one can learn and to which one can adjust.

I was born into what amounts to the upper middle class. My parents, through their hard work and dedication to saving, achieved many firsts in our neighborhood. They were the first to own a car. When television was introduced in my country, they were among the first families to purchase one. They achieved these dreams not because they were impulsive and able to buy fancy things with credit cards. They achieved these dreams because they had secured steady, well-paying jobs and were able to save the money they earned. It helped that they were well-educated compared to their peers; my father got his degree in commerce and banking, and my mother had been trained as a high school teacher. They were also highly religious, believing that with hard work, a higher power would provide for all their needs.

My fate was decided primarily because of my mother's and father's careers. Dad was an area manager for Barclays Bank. Mom was a teacher. Together this meant my parents knew a great deal about the significance of education for their children—and, more importantly, how to save for that education.

My father believed in a methodical and planned method of saving. He often said every working person should pay himself first—that is to say that he should put away a designated amount of money from his paycheck every month no matter what. Even if there are bills piling up that demand his attention, the savings account will be the first to receive funding. If he plans on saving $300 every month, for example, then at the first of every month he will take $300 from his paycheck and move it into the savings account. In this way he treats that money as if it doesn't exist—as if it isn't available for spending to begin with.

Dad also believed in disciplined investments. He invested in both the local stock market and tangible real estate. The latter point would prove especially fortunate for me when the American embassy initially declined my visa application. In response my family was able to use the equity in one of Dad's houses as proof and guarantee that we had the funds to sustain my American education.

My parents believed a college education—especially one in the United States—was a worthwhile investment in my future and theirs. In my home culture parents care for their children until they are old enough and financially solvent enough to flip the circumstances. Later in life the children of my country often take care of their parents when they become old and infirm. This cultural plan simply isn't possible without the ability to save. Unless a family has a nest egg, there will not be extra money available when it comes time to care for additional people in the household. In this way my own savings tendencies came equipped with cultural as well as familial demands.

To meet their goal to send me abroad for my education, my parents had to do without luxuries such as grand vacations, impulsive spending, new cars, or the best foods money could buy. These were luxuries they easily could have afforded on their salaries, but they prioritized their children's educations much higher. Such was their dedication that my mother once had to sacrifice her spare time to work part-time in addition to her regular nine-to-five job. My parents had made their plan and had placed my education abroad at the top of their list of priorities. This is another central tenet of saving like a

New American Millionaire: in business and in life, you must prioritize your expenditures.

By the time I was old enough to pursue secondary education, my parents had realized their dream. The money was saved, the house put up as proof of resources, and the embassy placated. The final task would be to choose my school. To this end my parents did as they often did: they fell back on their network of friends and colleagues to determine the correct course in life. Through this network they received a recommendation for the University of Illinois. It had served the sons of one of their cohorts well, and so they believed it would do the same for me.

New American Philosophy:
Take Advantage of Financial Opportunity

In my interviews with dozens of New American Millionaires, a common thread emerged when it came to the topic of raising and maintaining finances for an entrepreneurial endeavor: you have to take advantage of *every* financial opportunity you see. For many unsuccessful businesses, when money is tight the answer is often to call the bank and see if a new line of credit can be opened. For successful business—and almost always for the New American Millionaire—deepening one's line of credit is an absolute last resort. Even in the case where credit is necessary, the New American Millionaire never leverages more than he can reasonably afford to pay back within the first couple of years of business operations.

So what do I mean when I say "every financial opportunity?" I mean literally that. I mean you must be able to see opportunities to borrow or otherwise incorporate the funding and help of family, friends, and business contacts. Many entrepreneurs might avoid this possibility because of inherent pride, but pride alone rarely gets one ahead in this country. Often it is an obstacle to forging new alliances or otherwise building one's business. The truly savvy New American Millionaire is not above taking advantage of the many opportunities, both small and large, that are presented to him.

For Henry Wong, a prolific and successful entrepreneur, executive, and venture investor in the Silicon Valley for more than twenty-five years, making his early startups work following his emigration from China was a matter of stretching his personal resources to the limit. While he attended college, he shared a small apartment with his brother and kept his social life to a minimum. Like many successful entrepreneurs, he worked while he went to school. His job at an airline allowed him the advantage of being able to fly for free, which opened up opportunities to make business contacts across the country that might otherwise have been unavailable to him. In this way he was able to save money on his living and travel expenses—money he would later use to help found SS8 Networks, Inc.; IP Communications; XaQti Semiconductor; CNet Technology, Inc.; Combinet; and other highly successful technology companies.

According to Masoud Kermani, a structural engineer turned mega-entrepreneur, emigrating from Iran and starting a major consulting group was as much a matter of building relationships and recognizing opportunity as working hard and saving money.

"When I started Kermani Consulting Group, it wasn't the kind of business that needed materials or a lot of capital. It was more my idea. My biggest asset was my relationship with the people I met," he explained. As a man who began his career in the US as a structural engineer for a global engineering giant, the leap to real estate was certainly a risky one. But Kermani saw an opportunity to expand his wealth, and though he did not have as much experience or education in real estate he realized the market would allow him to turn a little bit of cash into a great deal of potential growth. In this way he could use his relatively meager savings to step onto a perceived path toward riches.

"In real estate I was able to buy properties and make deals to own homes just by taking over the payments without putting money down," he said. "But it was never the money that drove me. I respected money, but I wasn't attached to it. It wasn't my top priority in life, which is really what helped me enjoy my life no matter how much or how little money I made."

For Kermani, raising and making money is a matter of respecting money but not becoming so attached to it you start to believe it must always be growing quickly. Even if you don't perceive immediate growth it does not necessarily mean you're doing something wrong. "You have to be patient," Kermani advises. "You can't expect to buy a stock and watch it quadruple in five seconds. For everything in business, think long-term. Be patient and persistent. And always believe in yourself and keep a positive attitude."

Sometimes opportunity comes in the form of a perceived market need. For Gershon Mader, founding partner of Quantum Performance, Inc., starting his company after immigrating to Canada from Israel was not a matter of leveraging money but rather leveraging his business contacts into future opportunity.

"In the first four years in Canada, I worked at an American consulting company that was an expert in large-scale corporate transformations. I worked hard there to become more and more confident and effective in the methodology and techniques of the field. When it was clear to me that it was the right time to make the leap toward creating my own enterprise, I raised capital through securing future accounts."

Whatever financial advantages you see in your life, remember the task of properly leveraging money and help is a matter of your willingness to assume risk. "I remember when I first decided to leave," Mader recalls. "There was definitely some uncertainty if I would be able to pull it off.'" Risks like these require a certain boldness inherent in the New American Millionaire spirit, but they also require enough capital (or at least a low enough operating cost) to weather the occasional storm. For Mader, despite his best efforts at feathering his nest for the future, it took three months to secure the first project that would get Quantum Performance, Inc. on its feet.

You've learned already that to leave one's homeland requires substantial resources. A New American Millionaire can't obtain those resources without a keen sense of how to save and when to spend. Once the New American has established himself in America, the savings initiative does not stop. Fate favors those who are prepared, and those who know how to save are always prepared.

You have also learned that successful entrepreneurs rarely spend on credit. Companies that spend too rapidly or leverage too much often fail. Entrepreneurs who establish their businesses on low operating costs and sound financial principles are more likely to find success.

Few people know how to save. Even fewer know how to spend wisely. The following tips and tools will help you to learn this careful art and put it to good use.

The Three P's

New Americans tend to be better savers. The ideal savings plan adheres to what I call the three P's: plan, prioritize, and pay yourself first. If you can adopt these three P's, you will be better positioned to begin saving like a New American Millionaire. You will have all the tools you need to strike the perfect balance between responsible savings and moderate spending both in business and in life. You will move away from high-risk investments and toward more stable investment opportunities. You will learn to save wisely and create financial safety nets designed to help you and your business weather the occasional economic storm. In this way you will be able to build a financial nest egg that will improve your economic standing, drive your business, ensure your financial stability, and keep you on the path toward riches—much like the New American.

- **Tip #1:** Plan

  What I mean by *plan* is to create a budget. Too many entrepreneurs in the US—whether they're aspiring millionaires or otherwise—spend money on their businesses without any forethought. These people tend to pull out the business credit cards whenever perceived needs arise, then keep their fingers crossed when it comes time to balance the books at month's end. They might claim to have savings plans, but their savings accounts are often what I call *revolving door* accounts: they'll move $200 over to savings early in the month only to move it back to checking when perceived needs cross their desks. In this way they never build anything. Their businesses have every luxury they believe they need in the short-term, but there is no plan for the future and, as a result, very little opportunity for growth. Some fall into this trap unconsciously. Others are quite conscious of their problem but don't know what to do to escape the cycle.

The New American, on the other hand, tends to have fewer choices. He can't purchase that hot, new item for his business unless he has the money to pay for it. As a result his budget plan is often more detailed and better plotted than that of the spendthrift. Despite his often meager earnings and low startup capital, in the long run the New American Millionaire winds up with more money in the bank and more leverage to becoming successful in his market. It's not necessarily how much you make that makes you a millionaire; instead it's how much you keep that assures your financial status and business success.

The first step to planning like a New American is to rein in your spending. And the primary way to do that is to sit down with your company's financial records and create a spending plan that works on the bare minimum. Obviously the ultimate goal is to balance your budget. This means your expenditures should not exceed your income in any given month. Start by taking a look at last month's revenues. Add up the total and write the number down. The next step will be to list all of your expenses. Don't skip any, regardless of how insignificant they seem at present. We'll worry about prioritizing them in step two.

For now build a comprehensive list. These are your expenditures—the obstacles you must revise or overcome in order to build the total amount of money you can save each month. As you travel the path to riches, only your expenditures will hold you back. Let's move on now to the steps for minimizing the damage expenditures can cause.

- **Tip #2:** Prioritize
You now have a better understanding of your total revenues and a full list of expenses to reference. Looking at that list, you may now decide which among them are the most important. The New American Millionaire often has few choices. With a meager paycheck, the choice between paying for outside consulting and paying the electricity bill is a no-brainer. The New American Millionaire scrapes together the money needed to keep his business afloat, but then—assuming he prioritizes for the future—also sets aside money for the occasional dry spells to come.

For the American-born the choices are often more dramatic. Can you spend $1,000 per month on entertaining prospective clients? Maybe you can, but not at the expense of the electricity bill. You might make some nice contacts in that month, but by the end the utility company may shut off the lights on you.

Most people recognize the importance of prioritizing expenses, but few adhere to the principle. These people find themselves justifying unnecessary expenses as the month unfolds. They convince themselves of a need, do the math, and then attempt to make it work in their budget. This almost always leads to a loss of savings power and sometimes leads to a loss of credit if a person overextends his business dramatically.

But if you take the time to sit down and prioritize the expenses on your list, you will have a clear picture of the things that may be cut. It might hurt to cut them, but imagine the joy you will know on the day you become financially independent. I recall the day I first realized I had achieved financial success.

It had taken hard work and hard saving to get there, but the feeling proved unmatched.

So, do you need a $1,000 entertainment expense? No, probably not. Do you need that new company car? Not unless the old one is literally falling apart. Can you get by in a smaller office space? If the savings that result are attractive, then the answer is almost always "yes." Whatever the case, look at your list of expenses and prioritize them in numbers of two to ten (or one hundred, depending on your spending habits). Why should you begin with two and not one? Because the next tip should always be your number one priority.

- **Tip #3:** Pay Yourself First

  This is a concept I have already alluded to, and one my father took to heart from an early age. What I mean by *pay yourself first* is that the first bill you pay—that number one priority on your expense list—should be your savings account or other sound investment vehicle. It seems obvious, but try not to think of your savings as a burden; think of it as an investment in your company's future. You aren't paying another bill when you allocate a portion of your revenues to your corporate savings account. You're writing yourself a check. You're paying your future business.

  The most common approach to savings—and the one that works the least—is to create a financial plan and then, at the end of the month, move whatever money is left over into savings. The problem with this is twofold. First it all but guarantees that the amount of money saved will vary every month. One month you might save above and beyond your goal. The next month you might save far below.

  Second the problem with waiting until the end of the month to pay yourself is that it removes all motivation to improve your earnings potential. If you pay yourself first and assume the $500 (for example) you're putting into your business savings account at the start of each month is untouchable, then you now must scramble to make more money to pay your other bills. Your operating costs will be paid, but if you want to make a flight across the country to meet a prospective client, you might have to make a few extra sales to raise the capital. In this way you become more disciplined and motivated—if for no other reason than you *must* be disciplined and motivated.

The New American Millionaire is perhaps better equipped to meet this goal. Given his propensity to dream, he is always thinking of his future. And so his priorities are more likely to be to pay himself first. If you hope to succeed as he will succeed, you must learn to adopt this principle.

Using the three P's, I have managed to maintain a meticulously planned budget from the time I first began earning money in the US. By using a budget, I am able to identify clearly and easily my major expenses and cut back on those I deem less important. This way I can free up more money each month to save. In addition I maintain the discipline of paying myself first. Before paying any bills, I put away a predesignated amount of money in savings for myself each and every month.

New American Philosophy: The New American Millionaire Shortens the Runway

Many successful entrepreneurs are blessed with the good fortune of having access to a little money when they begin their business ventures. But, as many will tell you, even large sums of money tend to dry up quickly when it comes to startups. As Saeed Amidi, serial entrepreneur and founder and CEO of Plug and Play Tech Center, puts it, "You have to shorten the runway." You have to project how many months your business can operate on the funds available to you and then shorten that projection considerably. This is part of the reason savings are so important: no matter how much planning we do, we often fail to recognize every expense necessary to keeping a startup business running. For the entrepreneur there is never enough money early on.

For Amidi stretching those funds was a matter of keeping the overhead low. He started his company in a four-hundred-square-foot office equipped with little more than a desk and a telex machine. He did this because he knew his funding—generously donated by his father—would only last for six months. His father told him if he couldn't become cash-flow positive within six months, then the business would never last.

This is a lesson he has carried forward in all his business ventures. That runway to takeoff was six months for his first startup, and his rule of thumb has been six months ever since. This might seem like a startlingly short runway for most aspiring entrepreneurs, but there is a great deal of truth to it. Of all the New American Millionaires I interviewed for this book, none were still struggling to make sales or realize profits six months after startup. There were periods of financial difficulty, of course, but they were often short-lived.

So save (or raise) enough capital to keep your business running comfortably for at least a year, but understand the money will likely only last you six months—and if you are not cash-flow positive by then, your business might not be viable. At the very least, if you are not realizing a profit within the first six months, it is time to revise your strategy.

To recap, best practices for business spending and saving include saving more than you think you will need, shortening your runway to success, leveraging the people in your life rather than a bank loan, adhering to the three P's, and doing everything in your power to keep your initial operating costs as low as possible. Be sure to visit **www.milliondollarsuccessinstitute.com** for your free copy of a spending and saving spreadsheet that has worked for hundreds of entrepreneurs and will work for you too.

As a final piece of advice, remember that almost every business starts small and with very few resources. As Vinod Khosla, founder of Sun Microsystems, put it, "We are in the company [of] building business, not the 'deal' or 'capital' business." In other words you don't need all the money in the world to start a great company. You just need the aptitude. So be wise with what money you do have and patient with your expectation of growth. At the same time, work hard and with a sense of urgency, for if you are not seeing growth within the first six months, you may not make it. Finally, be sure to scrape every extra dime into your business savings account, for no matter how well things are going now, the climate in your market can always change.

In this chapter you learned how to spot and take advantage of all financial opportunities. You learned the three P's—the lessons that demonstrate how to plan, prioritize, and pay yourself first. Saeed Amidi shared his thoughts on shortening your runway to becoming cash-flow positive. With this wisdom you will have a greater chance of success when it comes to getting your startup off the ground or maintaining your existing business.

Ninety percent of all new businesses fail, and of that ninety percent a vast majority fails because of mismanaged funding. If you hope to avoid falling in with the rest who contribute to this dubious statistic, you must take the lessons of this chapter to heart. Take the steps necessary to make the three P's a part of your life and embrace the lessons shared by the successful CEOs who have come before you. Once you have done this, you will be ready to move on to the next chapter. There you will read lessons on how to minimize the fear inherent in launching a small business. You will learn how to assess and mitigate risk. Most importantly you will find a blueprint for becoming more like the fearless New American Millionaires.

cash-positive, but in retrospect he understands that
and less fear-driven approach might have sufficed
him up to address other matters of business growth
cess).

ay," he said, "any entrepreneur who needs to build a
hould start by communicating with the customers
o clarify their needs. Find out directly if you are
d able to provide the customer with what they seek,
e importantly, whether the customer is willing to pay

imple and direct approach tends to eliminate the fear
and the fear of "what if." There is no "what if" when
directly with the customer and lay everything out on

guing thing about fear is that once you have mastered a
ment, it tends to spring up again in a different form. For
ite the fact that my father and I were able to overcome our
everything to send me to America, I found a new kind
rriving in this country. The fear was derived from the fact
w a small fish in a massive pond. In my homeland I was
for my intellectual ability, academic achievements, and
ocial statuses. But in the United States, I quickly discovered
be anonymous. My achievements no longer mattered. My
ections disappeared. My social status was knocked down
No one I would meet in America would immediately know
kground or abilities. My relationships would begin with
text.

e me afraid of many things. Chief among those fears was
never fit in. In my darkest moments, I honestly believed
make new friends. Though I spoke English fluently, my
made it difficult to communicate. Often I would remain
for fear of being mocked or labeled and outcast. Where I
a master of higher learning, I now found myself struggling
tasks. Finding transportation proved a challenge. Finding

Chapter 4

Fearless: Falling Forward is Progress All the Same

The opposite of bravery is not cowardice but conformity.
—**Robert Anthony**

I AM SURE MY parents were aware their sweat-and-blood work ethic would be passed on to me. But I'm not sure they knew how their innate fearlessness would influence my early years in America. My parents were people of average financial means. They lived in a world where several of the component factors that define success were handed down from generation to generation. Just as blond parents tend to have blond children, so do fearless parents tend to have fearless children. Frankly this is the area of my upbringing for which I feel most fortunate: Right from the day of my birth, I was groomed for a life of success.

But, as I have said before, you don't have to be born with any of the eleven qualities that comprise New American Millionaire way of thinking. Good fortune and a keen interest in learning can close the gap.

When it comes to the quality of fearlessness—at least in terms of my intrepidity on the subject of making a new life in the United States—

my first bit of good fortune came when I reached high school, where I was afforded the opportunity to study under American Peace Corps volunteers. These teachers spoke endlessly about life in America. In so doing they often compared life in my country to theirs, always painting a picture of a land far more promising than my own.

I found myself particularly awestruck whenever my teachers discussed life at American universities. They spoke of the huge institutions, their excellent teaching amenities, and of course all the fun to be had on campus. For the skeptics among us, they even had pictures of the sweet life in America. If I wasn't convinced that my parents' idea to send me abroad was a good one before, meeting those American volunteers put me over the edge. I would study in the United States. And though the thought of leaving my homeland might cause many to cringe in fear, for me the decision was made.

Just before graduation—and on the strength of the exciting stories told by my American teachers—I applied to the University of Illinois. In less than a month, I received my acceptance letter. This was the day I learned that I would indeed be going to America. This was the day I finally had to put to rest whatever remaining fears I carried and make the commitment to get my student visa.

The American embassy was the first stringent requirement I would have to meet. For this reason I knew my acceptance letter did not mean it was time to celebrate. First I would have to pass the Test of English as a Foreign Language (TOEFL). Then I would need to travel to my state's board of education and attend an interview designed to weed out students not fit to travel. Finally I would need to take and pass various medical tests.

Though I passed each requirement with flying colors, the American embassy proved rigid and difficult to penetrate. It seemed that every time I thought I had met all my requirements, new protocol would spring up. At the end of the day, I was denied a visa pending further proof of adequate finances on the part of my family. While the embassy was satisfied with my abilities as a student, they apparently needed proof that my father could afford at least the first year's tuition and room and board at the U of I.

I mention this because I thin
bravery. Many parents, when fa
fold up their efforts, offended a
embassy. Not my father. He did
me. He knew if he worked at it h
dream, after all, to send his son t

Within the week we were re
documents in hand. Given that m
as proof of solvency, I was finally
defining moment for me. On this
the place of my dreams. I felt jubi
but apprehension about all the p
the first time, fear began to set in
our obstacles to my dream, but n
the leap?

New American Philoso

For an entrepreneur fear ca
damaging thing about it is that
into actions that aren't rational
to Saeed Amidi of Plug and I
lead an entrepreneur to overex
lesson the hard way back wh
company, which was an impor

"I remember I used to
received from overseas," he exp
Commerce would publish req
The publication would come ou
products. I used to go through a
the ten I thought I would best b

The key to overcoming fea
which fears are rational and wh
on ways to eliminate the latte
Amidi's herculean effort with tl
to establish a customer base th

compan
a simple
(and fre
in the p

"To
produc
directly
willing
and, m
for it."

Thi
of waiti
you spe
the tab

The in
particular
example, d
fear of risk
of fear upo
that I was
well-respe
familial an
that I wou
familial co
several pe
about my
very little

This
that I wo
I would
heavy ac
silent in
had once
with ever

food I actually enjoyed seemed almost impossible. Asking for directions to an unfamiliar building brought levels of stress I had never before experienced. My stress in general skyrocketed. My loneliness reached new heights.

But the primary fear factor for me was money. Most people don't realize the financial struggle endured by international students. Immigration laws require that international students be in school for nine full months before they may apply for a work permit allowing them to work off campus. This means scraping to get by on whatever one's parents can afford to send. For many there is the option of working on campus, but those jobs often pay minimum wage and restrict the number of hours per week that one may work.

The cost of tuition is different as well. At a junior college, a US resident will pay on average $12 per unit. For an international student, the cost is $140 per unit. At a four-year public university, the gap is even wider. While a US resident might pay between $1,800 and $2,000 per year, the international student will pay something more along the lines of $6,000 to $9,000. Couple this with an inability to work and that first year in the United States tends to look frightening.

I was determined not to allow the fear of uncertainty to overtake me. And so I pressed on. I did what I could to communicate, and I did what I could to earn money. I kept my head up and my eyes always looking forward. I tried to be just like my father.

New American Philosophy: Put Your Fear Into Perspective

When it comes to building a business, fear is perhaps the entrepreneur's greatest enemy. For the successful there are, of course times of fear, but it how they react to that fear can put them over the top and keeps their business going. Naren Gupta, a serial entrepreneur and founder of Nexus Venture Partners, puts it succinctly: "As a business owner, if you find yourself fearing an outcome, you have to ask yourself, 'What is the worst that could happen?'"

Fear is often a matter of living in the moment, of failing to recognize that life is long, fraught with successes and failures, and full of more opportunities than we can imagine. According to Gupta's lesson, if you fear failure you simply aren't recognizing that even the worst-case scenario in America is manageable for most.

"What happens if I fail?" he asked. "At worst I will have lost my business, my income, and my savings. I might have to give up my company and my dream in the short-term, but I can always go find another job, rethink my strategy, and begin again in several years."

"Things go wrong," Vinod Khosla, mega-entrepreneur and founder of Sun Microsystems, stated simply. "There is lot of uncertainty, and there are times when you're unsure of yourself." Khosla's advice is to spend less time swimming in the unknown. Pushing through the fear and guiding your business effectively is a matter of walking "this sort of schizophrenic divide between worrying that you're going out of business and dreaming big. Sophisticated entrepreneurs know this," he explained.

The best medicine for fear is the knowledge that failure is never the end of the road for a good entrepreneur. It is merely a new teaching opportunity—a new chance to learn how to reshape your business to become something better. "You learn a lot when you fail," Khosla reminded me. "It's a seemingly small nuance, but [failures] can make a huge difference in a company's trajectory."

Ric Fulop, of Northbridge Venture Partners and founder of six technology companies including A123 Systems, can testify firsthand about the healing power of failure. Some of his first technology companies didn't work out for various reasons, but he found the failures themselves were the best learning experiences—he can now see they were moments of clarity when he recognized the pivot points he needed to reshape his fledgling companies into good opportunities. As he said, "Good entrepreneurs are those who can use their failures to learn how to carve their paths in a market that is interesting and where they can create value."

When you rationalize your fear in this way, it helps you to deal with it more effectively. The key is to be daring, to go out and believe in yourself, to understand that failure is not an endgame but a temporary bend in the path of your life as a person and entrepreneur. Failure can seem huge in the moment, but it is never a permanent loss.

The act of carving out a life in a new country requires fearlessness. To champion a profitable company requires fearlessness. While fearlessness is often an inherent trait, bravery (which I define as a willingness to take risks) is something that can be learned. The following sections provide a number of steps you can take to improve your own willingness to take risks.

The Millionaire Takes Risks

Everyone takes risks every day. When you drive to work, you're taking the risk that you will arrive safely. When you cross the street, you're taking the risk of being struck by a car. When you meet someone new, you take the risk that he or she will be a negative influence in your life or career. These are the kinds of risks we all take for granted. So why then is it so easy to get caught up in a risk-averse spiral whenever a big business decision must be made?

Almost all entrepreneurs suffer this fate at least once in their careers. They simply can't decide what to do. The potential reward for a given decision could be huge, yet we find ourselves unwilling to take the leap. Before we delve into the steps for avoiding unnecessary risk-aversion, let me make one thing clear: you will never get anywhere if you never take risks. Your company's chance of growth will reduce substantially. Your chance of achieving financial success will diminish to zero. If you hope to achieve success, you must think like a New American Millionaire. You must imagine yourself as the New American considering whether to make the leap to the United States. If you do it, you are likely to find a life of greater luxury and opportunity. If you don't you may regret it for the rest of your life.

- **Step One:** Measure the risk

  Many people make the mistake of assuming that when they feel fear about a given decision, that fear is a result of the risk involved. Fear never stems from risk. It stems solely from uncertainty—and uncertainty can only come if you have not yet done your research. You must ask yourself, "What are the negative outcomes? If I go through with this decision, what are the chances I will fail? If I *don't* go through with this decision, what are the chances I will fail?"

  The second mistake most entrepreneurs make is to assume there are only two possible outcomes. This could not be further from the truth. Every decision has multiple choices—it's just that some are more easily spotted than others. It's important that you mete out all the potential choices because each choice comes with a different level of risk. It's possible that you might find a previously unforeseen choice to be more palatable than the more obviously available alternatives.

  Let's draw an example from your personal life. Let's say you cross an extremely busy intersection every day at lunchtime. This intersection doesn't have a crosswalk, but you take this route anyway because it saves you from having to make the trip in your car. There are statistics on the number of pedestrians struck at this intersection, and they show an alarmingly high rate of accidents—but you take the route anyway.

  It seems in this scenario that you have two choices: either you continue crossing the intersection or you don't. Continuing to cross means daily exposure to the risk of injury or death. Deciding not to cross means you are safer, but at the same time you will have to change your lunch arrangements, which could lead to unforeseen burdens on your time and money.

  Digging deeper, there are, of course, other choices. You could change your route to the same location. You could drive rather than walk. Or, my personal favorite, you could wear a helmet and body armor in order to cross the street.

Imagine you decide that you must cross this street in exactly the same way, but you can't afford to do it in your car. You now have two choices: walk the way you always have or take the safe route and wear the helmet and body armor. So outfitted, you might avoid losing your life if struck by a vehicle. Your chances of survival would still be low, but they would certainly increase with the helmet and the body armor.

Certainly there are other factors at play here. What's the level of reward for wearing the body armor? Not particularly high. If you're struck by a vehicle, odds are good that you will be injured or worse. And then there are the social elements to consider. If you were to suit up in body armor at work, you might find your coworkers giving you funny looks. Your social standing might diminish as a result of your paranoia. Under these circumstances wearing body armor and a helmet to cross the busy intersection seems absurd.

Now let's imagine you're suiting up in your helmet and armor to cross the same street, only now you intend to do so on a motorcycle. Socially speaking it's perfectly acceptable for you to wear protective gear now. You might even rise in social standing because of your risk-taking nature. But has your chance of survival when struck by a vehicle diminished? Not likely.

So you see how every risk carries its own weight and its own variance of outcomes. The only way to eliminate the fear often associated with this variance is to study the outcomes themselves and then rate them. When completing this exercise you will find that not only does every decision have more than two potential outcomes but those outcomes can be listed under different levels of viability as well.

Imagine now that you own a publishing company. For two decades your company has been perfectly profitable despite the fact that you have needed to outsource your printing process. Readership across the country is down, however, and your numbers have suffered as of late.

Unfortunately the printing company you have partnered with for all these years is suffering even more than you. They think they won't to be able to continue operations unless they can find an investor. You now have multiple choices on your hands. You may:

A) Search for another printing company to handle your needs, leaving your long-term partner to the wolves.
B) Purchase your own equipment so you can do your printing in-house from now on.
C) Acquire the failing printing company and merge their operations with yours.
D) Cross your fingers and hope for the best.

Each decision has its own level of risk. Each risk has its own uncertain outcome. Let's label each decision from one to five, with five being the highest level of uncertainty associated with the risk.

Option A is obviously the lowest-risk scenario in terms of process and finances, but it is perhaps the highest risk in terms of the business relationship. You might wind up saving money in the short-term, but your problem with the market as a whole will not be solved, and in the end you will have spurned a long-term partner. What if that long-term partner winds up building a new company that is far more profitable and in a position to help yours? How likely to help you will that new company's leadership be in your time of need? For these reasons we will label this risk a three.

Option B is elevated in terms of finances and process, as you will be saddled with the costs of buying printing presses and reorganizing your supply chain. The risk of spurning an old ally remains as well. For these reasons this risk should be labeled a four.

Option C maintains that high financial risk, but the process risk is lowered and the social risk reduces nearly to zero. For these reasons option C is a two.

Option D seems almost ridiculous now that we've covered the other three options. You maintain the status quo for now, but what happens if your partner fails? You're left without a printer, you fail to meet demand in the short-term, your supply chain falls apart, and you've done nothing to protect yourself from disaster. Waiting on your laurels, as is often the case, could be assigned risk level one or five. The question is: are you willing to leave the risk in the hands of fate?

However you decide to label your risks, when assessing an important business decision you must always ask yourself the following questions:

♦ How likely is it that this risk will lead to a negative outcome?
♦ How likely is it that this risk will lead to a positive outcome?
♦ What will be the level of impact if the negative outcome occurs?
♦ How much do I stand to benefit if the positive outcome occurs?
♦ What specific steps can I take to reduce the probability of the negative outcome?
♦ If the negative outcome does occur, what steps can I take to mitigate its impact?
♦ What is the outcome (whether positive or negative) if I do nothing and avoid the risk altogether?

When assessing your risk, try to remember that fearlessness isn't simply a part of the immigrant culture—it's a part of everyday life. If you think of your life as a timeline, it becomes clear that you have taken risks almost constantly. Growing up, making friends, falling in love, taking on business partners, assuming loans to launch your business, getting married, starting a family, raising children, buying a house—all of these things represented calculated risks that you readily accepted. Each probably caused you stress in the short-term, but where would you be if you hadn't taken the risk? Your life would certainly have been far less rewarding. And speaking of rewards…

- **Step Two:** Measure the reward
No risk assessment would be complete without a measurement of the potential rewards. In exactly the same way that you measured your risks, you must also measure your rewards. Again I propose a scale of one to five.

   Returning to our publishing example, the reward for option A is the potential to continue doing business in much the same way as before. You must alter your supply chain slightly, but most of your processes will remain intact. It's possible that you will be able to find a partner who charges less for the same services, but it's also possible that such a partner doesn't exist. The reward for option A is murky, so it should be assigned no greater than a three.

   Option B presents a potentially great reward in that moving your printing needs in-house will allow you to be more independent in the industry. It will also likely lower your operating costs long-term. Unfortunately it will also raise your operating costs tremendously in the short-term— and during a time when your business is already facing a cash-flow problem. While the risk is great for option B, so too is the reward. This is often the case with business decisions and exactly why the fearless often prosper. Option B presents a reward factor of five.

   Option C, much like option B, presents an opportunity for tremendous reward. It's true, however, that independence often leads to greater rewards than partnerships. Taking on your former ally would likely lower your production costs and would also bring you a motivated partner to help steer your company out of the darkness. Option C carries a reward factor of four.

Again option D is for the most fearful business owners. It is also unfortunately the path most take whenever they're faced with particularly difficult decisions. There is almost no reward for doing nothing—unless of course by some miracle the markets dramatically change and the problem fixes itself. Because miracles do happen, we can grant option D a charity point and call it a reward factor of one.

- **Step Three:** Narrow your options
Now that you have honestly assessed the levels of risk and reward for your decision, the choice becomes much simpler. Everyone holds different levels of fear, so you must decide how much risk you're willing to take on relative to the potential reward. In our publishing scenario, the choice remains difficult, but at the very least we may begin to weed out the less-obvious choices.

Option A, to search for another printing company to handle your needs, carries a risk factor of three and a reward factor of three. In this situation the risk is equal to the reward, so you must decide whether you are willing to roll the dice on what amounts to a 50-50 chance.

Option B, to purchase your own equipment and do your printing in-house, carries a risk factor of four and a reward factor of four. Again, high risk always comes with the potential for high reward. What's interesting to note here is that this is one of only two decisions where the risk factor is lower than the reward factor. For this reason it's important that you include this choice in your final deliberation.

Option C, to acquire the failing printing company and merge operations, carries a risk factor of two and a reward factor of four. Again we see a decision where the reward outweighs the risk. This choice should also make the final cut.

Option D, to cross your fingers and hope for the best, is only for the most fearful. The risk factor is either one or five depending on the eventual outcomes with your longtime printing partner and the market as a whole. The reward factor is a mere one. In this case the best you can hope for is a push between risk and reward. Hoping for best-case scenarios is rarely a sound business strategy. Option D may be eliminated.

Let's say for the sake of argument that you decide you are not willing to assume a risk factor of three just for the opportunity to obtain a reward factor of three. You aren't willing to take a risk that doesn't return a substantially better reward. Option A may therefore be eliminated. You are now down to two choices: take the riskiest road and acquire your own printing press or take the path of lowest risk/highest reward and acquire the failing printing company.

- **Step Four:** Listen to your intuition
  You might be saying to yourself, "That's still a difficult choice." This is true. The risk model is not intended to make every choice a simple one. In business, even more so than in life, there are no easy choices. The risk model is intended to eliminate choices that should not be left in consideration. Using our numbering system, we have done just that. The rest is up to you.

  When making business decisions, only the most fearless do not get caught up in a spiral of indecision. They listen constantly to their minds, which have the tendency to tell them one thing one minute and another thing the next. If you were the owner of the publishing company, you might find yourself waffling between options B and C. On the one hand, your long-term success would be better if you purchased the printing press. But could you survive the short-term financial crisis it would cause? On the other hand, partnering with your long-time ally would solve the outsourcing issue and lower your costs. But would you be able to work in a closer capacity with that ally?

  You see (and have likely seen many times) how the mind can complicate matters. For this reason, when faced with the toughest decisions, we must fall back on an often unheralded element of the human condition: intuition. Some people refer to it as "listening to your heart" or "going with your gut." Whatever the case, its importance should never be minimized.

You have completed all the actions you need to ensure you have eliminated all uncertainty. In other words you have gotten your mind in order—or at least as in order as a mind can be). If a clear decision has not been found, you must then turn to your intuition to determine the final outcome. To speak with your intuition, say the relevant statements dealing with each decision out loud to yourself, then assess how your body reacts. Pay close attention to your heart rate, your breathing, and any other sensation that may come up when you ask each question. For the purposes of this exercise, the following statements will be geared toward our publishing example. When you make your own statements to yourself, be sure to change the wording to reflect your unique decision.

- ◆ I will change the way I do business.
- ◆ I will alter my supply chain.
- ◆ I will purchase the materials I need to print in-house.
- ◆ I will acquire the printing company.
- ◆ I will do nothing.

Note what happens to your body when you make each statement. Many times it helps to return to this exercise several times over the course of a week. As new answers and variables present themselves, your intuition often takes different shape. Perform this exercise often enough and the answer will become clear.

- **Step Five:** Fear the right things
  They say our failures are never fully negative because they present opportunities to learn. This may be a cliché, but it's also true. Failure teaches us the greatest lessons, provided we are willing to study where we went wrong and take the steps to

ensure it never happens again. For this reason we cannot let the fear of failure get in the way of our decisions.

The best method of achieving this end—of becoming more fearless in the face of failure—is to turn the question around. Rather than fretting about your fear of a negative outcome, try to focus on what you might come to regret if you don't follow through with the choice you have made. If you can convince yourself your level of potential regret is higher than your chance of failure, what do you have to lose?

- **Step Six:** Take the leap

  The model above is obviously no guarantee of success. It is, however, an exceptional model when it comes to making your business decisions clearer. The final step to any decision—regardless of how you have come to assess it—is to take the leap and go through with your choice. It is remarkable how many entrepreneurs do their research and due diligence, then allow the opportunity to pass them by. That is unfortunate because you will never grow your business if you don't take chances. Even the ones that fail have a tendency to lead to the potential for new (and previously unforeseen) rewards.

  You have done your research. You have eliminated the uncertainty behind each potential choice. You have leveled your mind and listened to your intuition. Don't be fearful now. You have everything you need. Take the leap.

  The lessons learned from the New American Millionaires are clear: Assess your fears; determine whether they are rational or irrational; keep your fears in perspective; never let them dictate your decisions; and, most importantly, use the above risk assessment model to help alleviate your fears up front. At **www. milliondollarsuccessinstitute.com** I offer further solutions for how to navigate the risk/reward matrix in a way that is unique to your entrepreneurial field. With this tool and the lessons of this chapter, you will find yourself in a better position to make sound, reasonable decisions for your business—decisions based on logic and never on fear.

So you are now well aware that all entrepreneurs, successful or otherwise, experience some form of fear. Some are only occasionally aware of their fears. Some experience fear constantly. But as you will find in the chapter to come, the one thing very few successful entrepreneurs fear is the notion that they are somehow different from their peers. All New American Millionaires are outsiders by nature. They were born in countries other than the US, after all. Their cultural, linguistic, and social differences often cause them to stand out from the crowd.

The key for the New American Millionaire is not to assimilate. Rather it is to figure out how to leverage his outsider status to his benefit. He thinks outside the box by nature because he was *born* outside the box—and the ability to think outside the box is always a welcome trait in the entrepreneurial world. Read on to discover how, even if you aren't an outsider, you can enjoy the powerful benefits of thinking like one.

Chapter 5

Outsider: Thinking Like the Crowd Won't Get You Rich

*There is little difference in people, but that
little difference makes a big difference.*
—W. Clement Stone

PERHAPS ONE OF THE most underappreciated qualities of the New American Millionaire is his ability to use his status as an outsider to his advantage. For many the idea of being somehow different from the herd might seem like a terrifying prospect. But for New Americans and for successful entrepreneurs, being an outsider is akin to the kind of edge it takes to develop unique strategies, think outside the box, and separate themselves from the competition.

For the New American, being an outsider is a quality that's fully built in. I know this because I experienced it firsthand. During my early days at the University of Illinois, I was in a cauldron of intense emotion. There was, as I have mentioned, fear that I would never fit in to this new lifestyle, which was completely different from what I had known all my life. The other predominant emotion was hope that my circumstances in life would be better with an American education. But after the first few weeks of school, this emotion would often battle with uncertainty and confusion. I was a stranger in a strange land, and I couldn't help but worry about what would happen to me. The situations I encountered every day were not easy for me to handle. Aside from some physical hardships, I had many psychological and emotional troubles to deal with as well. Still, hope kept me going.

I think the first time I realized how much of an outsider I was came the first time I visited the university cafeteria. On the one hand, the food proved ample. On the other, it was completely different from my mother's home cooking. As I stood in line with tray in hand, I fretted about what I would order. These were exotic foods I had never heard of, let alone seen. What if I ordered something unusual? What if I ordered something I wouldn't like? What if I said something that would make people stare at me in that way they often did when I made a mistake of ignorance?

My answer to this dilemma was simple: I would order whatever the student in front of me in line ordered. Instead of braving the menu nomenclature—which was quite literally a foreign language to me—I would nod and say, "The same." The server would then plop down on my tray some strange food item I didn't even know how to begin to eat. Because of my fear of being an outsider, I virtually starved for the first month at school. I simply didn't know how to order my meals and didn't want to be scorned for my ignorance. Eventually I found relief by meeting other foreign students who taught me their own survival skills in this area.

On the academic front, my background was derived from the British system of education, which is remarkably different from the American tradition. Wont to writing my exams in essay form, I was thoroughly unused to the multiple-choice questions I faced on American exams. I recall receiving a D on my first psychology exam—a grade that came as a great surprise to me given my history of academic success. That D proved to be one of the most important lessons of my life, however, because it paved the way for me to learn that being an outsider isn't always a hindrance. In fact, if you can learn to use it, it can become a tremendous advantage.

Despite my initial struggles, I still believed in my academic capability and prowess. So I approached my psychology professor and explained my problem with this foreign style of exam-taking. He seemed to understand the dilemma at once, explaining that he remembered another international student who had experienced the same problem in the past. He was gracious enough to ask that I sit down in his office immediately and take a ten-question essay version of the exam. Upon completion I received a grade of A.

From that day forward, I came to realize that being something other than the status quo has its advantages. Outsiders can succeed in this country. In fact, if they know how to use their outsider status, they can succeed tremendously.

New American Philosophy:
The Outsider Doesn't Get Complacent

Sometimes being different can be an advantage simply because it requires you to change and better yourself. As Dame DC Cordova, CEO of Excellerated Business Schools, pointed out, "Every highly successful person who comes to this country from abroad has to take with them their foundation from where they learned and grew up. But also they have to educate themselves and adjust. They must know that these are their new circumstances and that they must work within these circumstances if they hope to succeed."

Often this means changing the way New American Millionaires live and work. The reason this change is so important is twofold. First, the simple fact that they have to change makes them more dynamic as people and professionals. They have, after all, mastered more than one way to meet any given challenge. Second, the necessity of change better ensures the New American Millionaire never becomes complacent. He gives his all to adapting to this new manner of doing things, and that teaches him firsthand that adaptation is always advantageous.

"In my practice, I have learned that people born in the US often become victims of their circumstances," Cordova revealed. "As a result they succumb to a standard of living they never dreamed they would have because they are not prepared with proper entrepreneurial education."

The New American's entrepreneurial education is built in to the task of immigrating to a new country. "When you come to the US under a diverse set of circumstances, you must go to work and learn how to adjust to what is given to you," noted Cordova. Much like the successful entrepreneur, you must be willing and able to adapt if you hope to survive.

For the New American Millionaire the role of outsider is often assigned early. The very act of considering transplanting oneself to another country requires the kind of outside-the-box thinking that turns an entrepreneur into a millionaire. It is often the case that anyone considering immigration does so primarily because he feels somehow different from his peers. Not coincidentally, this is one of the most frequent responses I received from the millionaires interviewed for this book—when asked how they would describe themselves, they often turned to negative arguments, claiming they "march to a different drum" or "play by their own rules."

A traveler to a foreign country, if he is to succeed in putting down roots in his new environment, must possess a balanced psychological and physiological outlook. Without it he will never survive his immersion into a foreign and often entirely different environment. He must have staying power—the ability to persist and persevere and to look at the big picture or ultimate goal instead of dwelling on the temporary shortcomings of his adjustment to the new country. He must maintain a strong, adamant desire to survive and overcome all obstacles.

Further, instead of relegating himself to the background, the New American Millionaire must get up and join the mainstream. He must start by shedding that spirit of being different and replacing it with making new friends and joining his hosts in new and unfamiliar activities. He must build and foster his fighting spirit—a spirit that keeps forging ahead in spite of the many rejections he will likely face. He must believe in himself and his capabilities. Only with self-confidence will he earn the confidence of the mainstream.

These qualities all apply to the up-and-coming millionaire entrepreneur as well. The entrepreneur will struggle until he learns to be persistent, maintain a fighting spirit, believe in himself and his capabilities, and truly embrace his role as an outsider. If he can do this, he will be well on his way to tremendous success.

Think Like an Outsider

We all feel a sense of otherness to one degree or another. There is good reason for this: no two people are exactly alike. It is not realizing your sense of otherness that will help you get ahead but realizing your ability to embrace that otherness and use it to your advantage. Few people have the emotional wherewithal to relish the thought of being an outsider. But with the following tips and tools, you may begin to establish what makes you different from the rest of the pack. It will be these differences, not your similarities, that will propel your business to success. Being an outsider is truly a position of strong value in a competitive marketplace.

- Outsiders work independently
  Because they are not subject to social and professional norms, outsiders are free to come up with their own plans and strategies. While an insider might find himself thinking along company lines, making decisions based on fear of negative outcomes, and doing whatever it takes to ensure his job is secure, an outsider is truly free from all of these shackles. An outsider brings value to the equation because he doesn't think like all the others. He isn't concerned with existing structures or plans. And his stake in the outcome is often lesser than that of the insider.

Couple all of this with the fact that outsiders often bring completely different skillsets to the table and you can begin to see why they are almost always considered valuable commodities. While everyone else spends their time trying to come up with old solutions to old problems, a truly independent thinker can provide new ideas. Their backgrounds are often so different and diverse they allow them to transcend the value offered by the comparatively vanilla insider.

- Outsiders think objectively
  When one grows up as an insider and works as an insider for a long period, one develops a series of natural biases. The insider knows how things are done because that's the way they've always been done. And if there is a shortfall in the objective, his biases cause him to assume it is the people at fault, not the process.

  Outsiders are not subject to such blindness. Because they come from different backgrounds, they operate with less bias. Where insiders rely on the patterns they have created, outsiders are particularly apt to see the shortcomings in those patterns. Again their lack of accountability within the organization or the market itself—the very thing that makes them outsiders to begin with—lends them the freedom to take risks where insiders wouldn't. The accountability is a two-way street as well. Insiders will be more willing to trust outsiders' decisions because they are that much easier to blame if things go wrong.

  In this way outsiders are more capable of finding new solutions to old problems. They see patterns emerge and work on ways to fix them. In the end their solutions are often far more likely to succeed than those of the insiders because they are fueled by a broader vision and a greater sense of independence.

- Outsiders operate unhindered
  Most insiders would have great ideas and do great things if not for the existing structures, which are often set up with

good intentions—but just as often they stifle creativity and productivity.

The simple act of working outside the organization or the market norms allows outsiders to be more creative because they aren't subject to the often rigorous structures to which their insider counterparts are subject. They don't have to meet protocol or play the political games associated with corporate culture or a competitive marketplace. They can do their own thing on their own terms. And this almost always leads to a better result.

New American Philosophy:
Embrace Your Personal and Cultural Advantages

Arjun Malhotra, founder of Techspan and Headstrong, once discovered a way to use some of the cultural norms of his upbringing in India to make an impact on his relationships with coworkers and clients.

"We do a great deal more entertaining at home in India than is typical in this country," he told me. Where in India it is normal to dine at home with a colleague or client, in the US such meetings always seem relegated to restaurants. The latter is typically a more sterile and impersonal environment than one's home. When considering this point, Malhotra had an epiphany that changing this dynamic would be an excellent way to use his outsider status to his company's benefit.

"'Why don't we just do it?' we said. 'Why don't we just invite our clients over to my house for a dinner meeting?' We knew right then that it would be a different experience for our clients. It would be something they would remember us for—something that would help us stand out from the other organizations attempting to get their business. And if we held our meetings in our homes, it might help us to build a different kind of relationship."

Malhotra details how he would invite major clients and prospects over to his home whenever they came to town for a visit. His wife would cook them a nice Indian meal. In this way the visitors would get a sense of the familial nature of Indian culture. This really seemed to stick—not simply because the initial culture shock was so memorable but because whenever a client or prospect allowed himself to settle in, he would see that families are the same everywhere in the world and that people who value their families are often the same people who value their business relationships.

"People are people wherever you go," Malhotra says. "Everywhere in the world, they are basically the same. If you treat them with respect, they will address you as equal, outsider or no."

How to Use Your Outsider Qualities to Your Advantage

You have already learned a number of advantages that outsiders tend to have over their insider counterparts. Now let's examine *how* to emulate that success. Let's determine exactly *how* to use your outsider qualities to your benefit.

- Take responsibility for yourself (and not for others)

  People who work for large companies have several major disadvantages compared to the outsider. First among them is that they are responsible for the well-being of more than just themselves. They have responsibilities to their bosses, their coworkers, their stockholders, and their customers. The work they do and the risks they take impact a large number of people.

  For the outsider no such predicament exists. If he fails at executing an idea, the only person he affects is himself. Plus, without all that responsibility—e-mails to respond to, bosses to appease, customers to call—he is free to exert all his energy on creating something new. While the insider spends his day taking care of his numerous responsibilities, the outsider is busy innovating. Insiders develop a routine designed to get through as many of their numerous action steps as possible in a given day. Outsiders operate in a perpetual state of being a single step away from achieving a goal.

So, to think like an outsider, you must work as if you are the only one who stands to lose. You must begin to think and work independently in all your endeavors. You must engage that spirit of confidence in yourself—a spirit that says, "I am the champion and architect of all my undertakings." Do this and you will begin working with more fervor and less worry. You will begin working as if you are free rather than lashed to a desk.

- Cast a wide net
  One of the most beautiful things about being an outsider is you are not obligated to focus on the tasks assigned to you. You don't need to spend all your time honing the specific skill or skills necessary to performing your job. You are free to do as you choose. You may learn as much as you like from other fields. And you may adapt to whatever new technology, structure, or niche arises.

  Being an outsider means working on a fair number of things at once. Don't get drawn in to one particular business venture or one particular innovation. Get as many irons in as many fires as possible. Learn from all you do. And, until you succeed in something, keep trying in as many different directions as possible.

- Do it smaller and cheaper
  Insiders, given that they work for well-established companies, have the luxuries of large audiences, large staffs with which to work, and much larger pools of funds from which to draw. This can seem like a benefit at first, but if you take a step back it's actually a hindrance. Because of these three factors, insiders are all but forced to create overly grand and large things. They must impress their audiences. They must expend the cash they have

afforded to them. And they must come up with as many things as possible for their employees and coworkers to do.

The outsider does not have to tie himself to massive projects. He is free to do things on a smaller and cheaper scale than the competition. Often this represents a distinct market advantage. Being able to offer a more cost-effective and easily produced alternative can be the quickest path to riches.

So, as an outsider, think on a grand scale but perform on a small scale. Study the competition to see what kinds of huge projects they have in the works. Then find ways to do the same things quicker, smaller, and cheaper.

- Use your time

  If you've ever had a desk job, you're already well aware of how scheduled that kind of life can be. The insider's day is full of expectations—places to be, people to meet with, tasks to complete. Outsiders do not suffer from this affliction. Because there is no one counting on them, they are free to delegate time elsewhere (or even procrastinate) on anything they like.

  For an outsider life is a little like being in college. There are many tasks to complete—tests to study for, papers to write, social obligations to attend to—but despite all that there is more time than he knows what to do with. While the insider tends to his day job, pays his bills, and returns home to his family, the outsider coasts through the day, completing whichever tasks seem the most imminent.

  Gaining an advantage here is simple because you have more time on your hands than your insider counterparts. Use it wisely by prioritizing your obligations in the order of their importance. And enjoy it while it lasts.

- Find your audience

  As I previously mentioned, insiders have the distinct advantage of having access to larger audiences. An established cable company, for example, has hundreds of thousands and perhaps even millions of subscribers while a cable startup is perhaps still going door to door. The good news is that the gap is closing.

Thanks to the Internet—the great democratizer in terms of audience—it is easier than ever for a small company to be seen and heard. Outsider products and services have a way of exploding into tremendous popularity overnight. This levels the playing field in more ways than one. First the outsider has access to a massive audience he didn't have access to before. And second, because of this access, the outsider no longer has to mimic the tactics of the competition in order to get ahead. YouTube didn't need to lay cable in order to take market share away from Comcast. It simply had to start broadcasting its own content for free.

So take advantage of this new and exciting fact. You have access to the same audiences your larger competition enjoys. Find them, determine what they like, and market to them in ways that the insiders haven't yet considered.

- Think on your feet
Insiders almost always have to follow protocol in order to achieve predetermined outcomes. Their bosses or their audiences have told them what is expected of them, and now they must work with their heads down until those expectations are met.

Not so for an outsider. Since nothing is truly expected of him—indeed, he operates so far on the fringe that most people don't even know he exists—he is free to make things up as he goes. He may set out to achieve one outcome only to discover that an entirely new outcome could be more effective or profitable in the process.

As an outsider you are free to try whatever you like. The simple act of trying expands your innovative horizons so dramatically it's difficult to overestimate its value. Your status as an outsider allows you to be a free thinker. So think freely. And don't be afraid to change things as you go along.

- Take risks

  Speaking of fear, this final point harkens back to the previous chapter. An insider isn't able to take the same kinds or the same levels of risk as an outsider. As mentioned in the first point of this segment, the outsider is responsible for no one but himself. If a risk doesn't pan out, who has he hurt? So, if he can begin to develop that bravery discussed in the previous chapter and he can appreciate the freedom his outsider status affords him, he is destined to do great things.

  Your competition is bound to take the most conservative route possible in order to keep their jobs. Don't follow the same path. Take leaps. Make mistakes. Learn. Execute. And always look for that next opportunity to try something new.

Being an outsider allows you to maintain an edge over the competition. Oftentimes outsiders see things others cannot. In turn they use those things to their advantage in the workplace and the marketplace.

Assess your own line of thinking about work, marketing, fundraising, product positioning, and any other aspect of entrepreneurship you may need to start your company. Once you've made that assessment, determine ways to make your thinking and your approach different from all the rest. Don't get complacent with your methods and plans. Use your personal or cultural differences to get ahead of the competition. Follow the steps to becoming an outsider, embrace the role, and watch your business begin to expand as a result.

Once you have absorbed the lessons of this chapter, you will have reached a better understanding of the valuable differences you bring to the table for your business, for the marketplace, and for your prospective clients. If you can continue evolving as an outsider, remain independent, and continue thinking objectively, you will find yourself with the kind of unfettered freedom it takes to succeed in an often cutthroat entrepreneurial world. With those lessons in mind, you will have a better understanding of who you are as an entrepreneur and what specifically you bring to the table for your unique business. The next step in the New American Millionaire evolution is to discover and grow the passion that will drive you toward success.

Chapter 6

Passionate: The Ultimate Evolution of Napoleon Hill's "Burning Desire"

Success is the good fortune that comes from aspiration,
desperation, perspiration, and inspiration.
—Evan Esar

WHEN I USE THE term *passionate* as the title for this chapter, I am referring to a drive to succeed. The assumption made when it comes to American success is that obtaining wealth is the only means of succeeding. While I posit there are many other avenues to success—and therefore many different versions of the burning desire about which I intend to write—monetary success is indeed the heart and soul of this book. So, in a way, with this chapter I am urging you to embrace your burning desire to achieve riches.

Anyone who hopes to get on the path to riches in the United States must harbor a passion for financial success. And New American Millionaires are particularly apt to demonstrate how that passion works. One of the top reasons for immigration, as cited by immigrants, is a desire to earn more money in a land that better affords them the opportunity. Those who rise to the top—those who come to champion companies like Google and Yahoo!—do so at least in part because their desire is greater than that of the competition. Anyone can say they want more money; it's the truly hungry who go out and make their businesses work.

For the New American Millionaire, that desire is developed from an early age. It is often born of poverty experienced in their home countries (and continued during their first years as aspiring Americans). It is then nurtured by that sense of otherness described in the previous chapter. When faced with such otherness, the New American Millionaire has two choices: he can cave in and return to his home country or he can redouble his passion to succeed in the United States.

New American Philosophy: Never Surrender

Many times what separates the successful entrepreneur from the unsuccessful one is that the former simply does not know the meaning of the word *quit*. Even when times seem dire, even when there seems to be no hope that his business will ever raise the funds it needs, make the sales it needs, or reach the customers it needs to reach in order to get off the ground, the successful entrepreneur does not give up. He keeps fighting in the face of improbable odds.

The same is often true of a New American. One could make the case that New Americans never surrender out of necessity (in many instances even when they struggle to make ends meet, they have no alternative but to remain in this country and keep trying to make enough money and advance their lives in a positive direction) or out of inbred spirit. If they hoped to save the money and clear the hurdles necessary to come to the United States, New Americans had to work hard and never give up. People like that have the "never surrender" spirit built right in. Theirs is a burning desire born of their circumstances and their upbringings.

According to serial entrepreneur Henry Wong, burning desire is absolutely critical to entrepreneurial success. "It is the energy inside you that drives you to succeed," he explained in our interview. "I have seen many entrepreneurs who walk away from their ideas and surrender. And I've seen others who never give up because they have faith in their idealism. That's the attitude you should have in starting a business. You aren't looking simply to advance an idea or make money off the soup of the day. You're looking to make a great concept a reality."

Sometimes making an idea into a reality requires us to look beyond our petty struggles and maintain our beliefs in ourselves and our dreams. When faced with debt, difficulty, and even financial disaster, giving up is always the easy thing to do. Those who succeed are often those who refuse to throw in the towel.

I am living proof that passion is essential for overcoming early obstacles in business and in life. For me the story began with the immigration process. Some of the barriers I faced in the first year included culture shock, distance from my family, and adjusting to American English. But all of these factors paled in comparison to my need to find the money necessary to continue my college education. My lack of financial options made my new university a very expensive home away from home.

As an international student, I couldn't receive US government money or take out student loans. I had to pay extra for insurance and cost-of-living needs simply because my parents did not live down the street. And, worse yet, I had to scrounge for the few on-campus jobs left after the flurry of phone calls from alumni demanding to secure such jobs for their children. These restrictions left me with few viable options. If I wanted to succeed, I simply had to be hungrier for success than my American counterparts.

This passion manifested in a great number of inquiries into jobs on campus. But even as I made headway, another hurdle surfaced: I discovered I would need a Social Security number in order to be employed by the university. There is a strange catch-22 associated with this dilemma as well: you can't have a job without a Social Security number and for most non-citizens of the US, you can't apply for a Social Security number unless you have a job. So finding work became tricky.

Despite the financial hardships (to say nothing of the bureaucratic difficulty of obtaining a Social Security number), I pressed on. I found renewed courage whenever I remembered the great citizens of my country, even a past president, who had to endure this same rigor to get an American education. With mixed feelings of dejection and determination, I continued my search and eventually landed a temporary, on-campus job busing tables after school. My burning desire to succeed got me to the point where I could keep my head above water. The question then became: would it be enough to sustain me?

Many would suggest people with a burning desire for success—those entrepreneurs like Henry Wong, who refuse to give up—are possessed of that necessary passion because they were born into environments with good work ethics and passions for success. If one is born into poverty or perhaps into a culture with few entrepreneurial opportunities, one has little choice but to work as hard as possible in the hope of rising above it. For many this breeds an inherent burning desire. The question is: can it be learned?

My research suggests that yes, a burning desire can be learned. While some entrepreneurial traits are inborn, passion for success can be developed with practice and care. Observe and absorb the following tips and tricks; make them a part of your everyday life and you will have what you need to stay hungrier than the competition.

How to Build a Burning Desire
- Think and live positively
  Those who positively believe they will achieve success are far more likely to reach their goals. Part of what makes the New American Millionaire spirit is a sense that being in America, the

land of opportunity, means no matter what happens, success will come to those who work. This is an overwhelmingly positive message—the veritable fuel for the burning desire. Staying positive even in the face of difficulty is therefore an essential component to passion.

According to Masoud Kermani of Kermani Consulting Group, when it comes to burning desire, positivity is paramount. "My motto in life and in business has always been, 'What kind of service can I provide?'" Kermani explained. "Having a burning desire is necessary, but having a positive attitude and the right morality (or at least the ideas that you can't hurt people on your way to your goal and that you can't seek money at any price) is even more important. If you push your burning desire for success too much it becomes greed, and greed is rarely a component of ultimate success."

With Kermani's wisdom in mind, let's explore a few tried and true methods of achieving a more positive mindset. For starters you might consider using inspirational books, audio programs, and videos. If you want to enter into a new market, absorb all the how-to information you can on it. You can surround yourself with positive visual reinforcements. If you have a sales goal, create a graphic that represents the progress on that sales goal and post it on the wall in your office. Every day you make progress, update the graphic to reflect it. In this way you can literally see how far you have come and how far you have yet to go. Finally, surround yourself with only the most positive people.

Most people interact on a daily basis with at least a few predominantly negative people. They tend to permeate working environments. The best approach is to take steps to cut them out of your life. If you have goals that seem lofty, stop sharing them with those who would respond derisively. Meanwhile ally yourself with people who are willing and apt to encourage you about your goals. These people should be the types who always ask about your progress, offer encouragement, and even volunteer to help. Bonus points if you can ally yourself with people who have already achieved the goal you're setting out to achieve. These people serve as a constant reminder that what you're doing is possible—and they often have a wealth of valuable advice to provide as well.

Finally, work to cut out all the negative influences in your environment. If your home or office is messy, clean it up (and keep it that way). If you have a tendency to watch depressing television programs—like the news, for example—consider changing your viewing habits. And it goes without saying, but if you have any bad habits like excessive drinking or smoking, you should take steps to drop them. These might seem like surface steps—mere window dressing—but they are in fact essential to the process of breeding a burning desire for success. Success means happiness, but it is not the only source of happiness. It is far easier to achieve success if you are happy to begin with.

- Lose the excuses and start committing
  In keeping with Henry Wong's point about never giving up, the single greatest hindrance to the *burning* portion of *burning desire* is the natural human tendency to create escape routes. If you set up a goal to meet a certain sales figure by a certain date, but then don't achieve that goal, you might find yourself making excuses. "Well, the economy declined this quarter." "The competition just rolled out that new product." "I was sick for part of July."

  Making yourself believe in these excuses is natural. It's part of how we deal with failure. We give ourselves escape routes from our toughest battles so we don't find ourselves facing certain letdown. But these excuses, these escape routes, are your number one obstacle to breeding that burning desire. If you're willing and able to run for the nearest exit as soon as things start to look bad, you'll never achieve the full and satisfying success you're hoping for.

The first and most important step to becoming one of the hungry is to eliminate your escape routes. Don't give yourself excuses. Make them disappear. Instead of telling yourself you hope to make a certain sales goal for the next quarter, set yourself up with actual consequences for not achieving that sales goal. Remember, the New American doesn't have any excuses. If he fails to make it in America, he doesn't have such an easy escape route. He might find himself without money, a job, a Social Security number, or a way home. Knowing this, he works harder than most to achieve his goals. And he will gladly apply that same passion to his business ventures.

- Visualize your success
  It's one thing to dream about a better future. Burning desire calls for you actually to *see* it. There are many books on what it means to visualize success and how such techniques can work to build a more positive reinforcement of self-image and personal drive. The reason for this is simple: visualization *works*.

  The next time you're feeling beaten down by your obstacles—the next time you feel like your dreams aren't achievable—try this: pick out your favorite (and preferably most inspiring) music and listen to it for twenty minutes. It can be a particularly inspirational album, song, or classical piece. Find a quiet place free of distraction, start the music, close your eyes, and imagine yourself having already reached your goal. If your goal is to become the market leader in your area of business, imagine yourself sitting in a plush leather chair in the corner office of your new building. Imagine yourself leading meetings, inspiring your employees, and gaining market share. Imagine yourself driving the car of your dreams, living in the house of your dreams, and enjoying a more fulfilling life.

  Try to make these images as true to life as possible. As you listen to the music, think of the colors in each scene. Think of what you might say, who you might encounter (and what they look like), and what you might smell, taste, and touch. Truly embrace the exercise. Do not do this halfway. Do not give up in the middle, assuming the exercise will have no effect on you. Believe me, it will. In fact it already works on you every day. This is the exact same method employed by every television commercial you've ever seen. The colors are always bright, the images always vivid, the people always lovely and expressive, and the music always catchy. This is the way to program your mind to desire something. If you can program your own mind in the same way a commercial conditions you to favor a given product, your burning desire for success will become inherent.

What you're doing when you listen to your music and imagine a brighter future is not simply daydreaming; you are beginning to associate your chosen music with this positive mental reinforcement. Essentially you're turning your favorite and most inspirational music into a tool you can use to change your mood in the face of adversity or negativity and add fuel to your burning desire. Scientists call this process *neuro-linguistic programming* (NLP), and it has worked for many on their paths toward riches.

Once you have programmed yourself to feel positive reinforcement when you listen to the music, consider beginning every day in this way. Listen to the same music for a week or two. Then repeat the exercise with a new album, song, or classical piece. Retrain your mind to achieve that same positive reinforcement from different music—and, of course, update your visualization of the future based on the progress you have made to date.

• Dress the part
Now that you have a clear picture of your ideal future, ask yourself this one important question: what kind of clothing was your future self wearing? Were you in an office behind a sharp mahogany desk? And if so, were you wearing a tracksuit? Of course you weren't. You were wearing a powerful business

suit. So why would you wear a tracksuit while still in pursuit of your dreams?

"Dress for success" may be a cliché, but it works. The more you go to work in sweatpants, the more you will perform like someone in sweatpants. In such comfortable and work-inappropriate attire, you will be closer to a burning desire for sleep than a burning desire for success. Wear nice clothing. Wear clothing that makes you feel powerful and in charge. Do this and you will be startled by how much better you feel. Your self-image will have no choice but to become more positive. Every time you look in the mirror, you won't just hope for success— you'll see it. Do not underestimate the power of such things. Burning desire isn't possible without a positive self-image.

- Get to work

  One of the single greatest mistakes entrepreneurs make is setting goals and then spending the next few months and years revising the plan. The New American doesn't revise his plans— he determines them from day one and acts on them every day thereafter. If you do not do the same, you risk falling behind.

  Too many entrepreneurs make plans and then never follow through because they feel like they cannot begin until the plans are perfect. Always remember the path to success is ever-changing. If you spend all your time watching for and anticipating the changes, you will never make progress. You will be stuck at the start of the path, unable or unwilling to continue. So, dream big and plan big, but don't let your big plans overwhelm you. Focus on the small things you can do each day to help you further your dreams. Avoid dwelling on the potential for failure. Just act. And don't adapt until it's absolutely necessary.

  Sometimes the greatest fuel for burning desire is simply action. Goals are never achieved without some sense of momentum. If you allow your momentum to waiver because of a perceived need to rethink or revise," you run the risk of losing it entirely. Nothing undermines desire like overplanning and procrastination. So stay focused on the task at hand. Get things done. And before long your desire will be such a part of you that you will think of your success not as a dream, but as a given.

As you have seen, passion is a matter of positive reinforcement and careful dedication. If you are willing to absorb the strategies listed in this chapter, you will find your desire building exponentially. Every success will only add fuel. Every setback will be overcome. You will find yourself acting as a New American Millionaire—the kind of person with passion and burning desire; the kind of person who can't help but succeed.

In this chapter you learned never to give up, to think and live positively, and to set aside your excuses and commit to what must be done. You gained insight into how to stop dreaming and start living your life as a successful entrepreneur. Now all that remains is for you to do the work it takes to make your vision a reality. When you align your strategies with your vision, and when you take all the lessons of this chapter to heart, you will be ready to begin formulating your strategy for how to take your business to the next level. As you will see in the coming chapter, that strategy requires you to embrace your sense of adventure.

Chapter 7

Adventurous: Life's Own Key-to-Everything

*Man cannot discover new oceans unless he
has the courage to lose sight of the shore.*
—Andre Gide

ENTREPRENEURS IN GENERAL ARE what I like to call a *different breed of the same caste.* They are persistent, smart, daring, and, most importantly, hard-working. They are also given to optimism; bold; extremely skilled at their chosen niches; and energetic.

New Americans, on the other hand—particularly those who find themselves carving out their paths as entrepreneurs—tend to exhibit additional entrepreneurial traits peculiar to their immigrant experiences. These traits include the fact that they are well traveled, multilingual, can offer diverse ethnic vistas to a given task, and are possessed of a great thirst for adventure.

Adventure is perhaps the root of the entrepreneurial spirit. One simply will not be willing to face the risks inherent to any startup business if one does not have a keen sense of adventure. To be adventurous *is* to be a risk-taker, but it also *is* a matter of being able to look into the future and forecast success. To be adventurous one must be able to see the positives of the end result and be willing to take the risks necessary to achieve that result.

One must also be willing and able to let go of all the common excuses that drag the un-adventurous down. The adventurous does not believe there is a better time for this opportunity. He does not believe there is not enough money. He does not believe other people are brighter or better suited to meet this adventure than he is. He simply recognizes that there is an opportunity before him, that he is talented enough to meet it, and that the time to pursue it is now.

The entrepreneur is adventurous because he is not just willing but *compelled* to forgo the safe route—that office job with a steady paycheck, benefits, and a nice pension—in order to blaze a new and more lucrative trail. For the New American Millionaire, the adventurous spirit is much the same. He must be able to dream of a brighter future in a freer culture and be willing to take all the risks associated with traveling to and making a life in another country. Generally his sense of adventure emanates from his innate curiosity. Often New Americans are driven by a perpetual need to explore and learn as much as they can about the people and cultures around them.

The adventure of my life story began on the day I first traveled to the United States. But as I have discussed, my adjustment proved quite difficult. I discovered the hard way that tough times tend to separate the adventurous from all the rest. For me it became a matter of adapting, failing, or doing something daring and new.

Life on campus at the University of Illinois was becoming drudgery. I had made very few friends and little headway in the classroom, and I was struggling to make ends meet. On the whole I did not feel like my experience to date was enough to excite my passions. The loneliness proved pesky. I continued to feel a gnawing sense of not belonging. Money was scant. I woke up every morning feeling like I was not meant to be there and no matter what I did nothing would ever improve. Depression had set in.

But, like many American adventurers who had come before me, that depression led to a longing for change—and that longing led me to start looking west. Opportunity came calling. I knew very little about what my future would hold, but I did know a city called San Francisco in the state of California would be my next stop.

I learned there were new opportunities in California from my aunt, who had immigrated before me and made a life for herself there. Over the phone she told me about all the things I could come to expect in this exotic state. Although she admitted life was not exactly a bowl of cherries for her, from our talks I gathered California might have offered more opportunities for me than Illinois. The glittering cities, the diverse population that represented almost all parts of the world, the foreigner-friendly Californians, the Golden Gate Bridge, and the great universities all sounded to my New American mind like the proverbial land of milk and honey. By the time my aunt had finished answering all my questions, I knew where my next adventure lay.

I found myself nervous and excited in the months leading up to my trip to California. There were too many unknowns, which sparked fear. I had heard a rumor that big American cities could be dangerous—rife with crime—and my young mind latched on to this idea. This, after all, was the old and Wild West. In my imagination I would land in California and find that everyone walked the streets toting guns in cowboy fashion.

On the day of my move, as I pondered the good and bad about my destination, an unsettling feeling pervaded. I wanted so badly to join my aunt in California, but at the same time anxiety enveloped my whole being. It stemmed from this: I had set out on an adventure once before, and it had cost me a great deal in terms of pride, money, and happiness. How could I be sure that taking a second, similar adventure wouldn't lead to the same depressing outcomes?

In the end my sense of adventure won out over my uneasiness. Feeling beads of sweat running down my face, and with my few university friends by my side to say their farewells, I took a deep breath, calmed myself down, and stepped into the bus station on West Carroll Street. As the bus departed, I felt slight regret and a pang of nostalgia as I watched my friends retreat into the distance. Doubt lingered only for a short time, however. It was soon overwhelmed by excitement.

The journey westward filled my heart with a renewed sense of why I had come to this great land. The bus ride afforded me the opportunity to take in the sights and sounds of many different cities and states of this great country. By the time California made itself known on the horizon, I found myself reeling with excitement at all the adventure and possibility that lay ahead. I would have a new school, a new job, a new home; and, in a few hours, I would see my aunt for the first time after many years apart.

My willingness to trek confidently into the unknown had been born in part from my thirst for adventure, which had been ingrained in me during my upbringing. I grew up in a family that shunned cowardice and extolled courage and bravery in the face of adversity. That thirst was developed further by a sense of desperation. It seems most of the great adventurers embarked upon their journeys out of need—for a better life, for greater opportunity, for more money. These are the things that drive the pioneer, the entrepreneur, the immigrant, the adventurer, the millionaire. For me the desperate fact was I had flown and landed here and had found suffering where I had expected to find success. This sparked my thirst for adventure, and I became determined to make a great new life for myself by whatever means and cost. I simply could not fail. As far as I was concerned, the bridge that would take me back to my home country had been burned. There would be no going back without victory. I had to succeed or perish.

For Arjun Malhotra of Techspan and Headstrong, the spirit of adventure was a trait thrust upon him by political circumstance. Born in India, Malhotra grew up in a country of thriving entrepreneurial spirit because so many of its citizens had grown up as refugees under British rule and partition.

"My parents worked hard to build a middle-class life for us," he explained. "We grew up in an environment where nothing in life was taken for granted and where entrepreneurship was celebrated in the same light as personal freedom. Many of us grew up willing to take risks and be adventurous because we didn't want to share the fate our parents had experienced in their early lives."

Entrepreneurship is itself an act of adventure. More often than not, succeeding as an entrepreneur—and becoming one of America's wealthy few—is a matter of being more adventurous than the competition, of always having the courage to follow one's heart into the unknown. Some people are more adventurous than others. Fortunately that same spirit can be learned. The following tips and tools will help you to see better where the potential for adventure lies in your own life. Embrace them and you will find yourself more willing to harness your adventurous spirit and seize upon opportunities that could lead to great success.

How to Be Adventurous

- Get out there

  If you are stuck in a rut, lonely, bored, or feeling unfulfilled, then it is time to change something about your life. In business, if things seem to stall, it's because you have not yet made enough contacts or reached enough people. Sometimes being adventurous is simply a matter of shaking things up. Attend a conference. Make some calls to influential people. Walk straight into the office of a potential business partner and set up a meeting. At **www.milliondollarsuccessinstitute.com,** I offer a link to connect entrepreneurs searching for insight or aid from their fellow entrepreneurs. This online networking community will surely help to point you in the right direction of the people who can help you and the seminars or conferences you might consider attending.

  If you have an idea for a new business, start putting the word out. Do not return endlessly to the planning phase. Take action. Introduce yourself to as many people as possible. Build a website. Start advertising. Visit with and speak to as many people as possible about your idea. See what people think. Your idea will never go anywhere if you never leave the garage. Talk, introduce yourself, advertise, and take chances.

The more people who know about your idea, the better your chances are for success.

- Set goals
  It seems trivial, but sometimes adventure can be daunting. The best way to keep yourself on track is to leave little reminders of the progress you have made. Set goals and then work to meet them. Your goals can be big (build an alliance with the market's top performer) or small (buy photo paper for flyers), but be sure to look to them always. The most important goal to meet is to achieve something every day. It can be anything. Just work hard to ensure every day is more fulfilling, exciting, and productive than the last.

- Take action
  Doubt can damage a dream in numerous ways. It's particularly devastating when it leads to indecisiveness or inaction. In business the first to market gains the spoils. Do not miss out on your opportunity because you have doubts. There is no time to wait. You've seen an opportunity. It's quite possible there are other people who have seen that same opportunity. The time to implement is now.

  Gershon Mader of Quantum Performance, Inc. is no stranger to the concept that one cannot allow doubt to get in the way of action. Having grown up in Israel and served as a captain in an elite commando combat unit, he has lived a life of quick decision and decisive action. He has translated these qualities well in his consulting business; he often finds the difference between success and failure in a given exercise is a matter of taking action in the face of doubt.

  One story he shared with me holds particular weight. The nature of Mader's business is coaching, consulting, and empowering executives and teams to assume bolder futures and ambitions, to address challenges and issues, and to build stronger levels of cohesion between people. In many ways his job is a matter of making people become more adventurous in the way they envision and perform their work. And it is often an adventure to get people to communicate with one another openly, honestly, and courageously.

One of the most pivotal moments in Mader's career came when he was attempting to smooth out the differences between a particularly curmudgeonly high-level executive and his highly unionized staff. The important thing to remember about this particular executive is he was the decision maker on a multimillion-dollar account for Mader's company—a deal that would have made or broken Quantum Performance, Inc. in its early days.

After months of working with the executives and other decision makers at the company, Mader was finally able to convince the top executive to allow his staff to express their thoughts openly about his management style and how he might improve as a leader. The task called for Mader to assemble in one room more than a hundred key people who worked with and for the top executive. He would then have to sit in front of this crowd and listen to how he might become a better manager.

Now this would be a difficult experience for anyone to endure, but for this particular executive the session proved intolerable. After a time he grew so angry he stood up and stormed out of the room. Everyone sat in stunned silence for a moment before Mader put aside all doubt about offending his top client and sprang into action.

"Not even thinking about right or wrong," Mader revealed, "I ran out of the room after him. I stood in front of him in the hall, physically barring his path."

The important thing to remember here is that this executive represented a multimillion-dollar take for Mader's company. And yet there he stood, holding his client back and arguing with him about returning to the room to finish what he had started.

"I explained to him that if he left the room, he wouldn't be living up to what he told his staff," Mader said. "It might have been a risky move, and I might have had my doubts if I had stopped to think about it, but I was simply not willing to let my client trash everything he had been trying to build for six months."

In time the executive began to listen to reason. To Mader's great surprise and relief, he returned to the meeting and allowed it to continue. In the end Mader's action caused the client to achieve the goal he'd had in mind when he'd first hired Quantum.

"That experience taught me not just the courage of adventure, but of taking action and doing the right thing," said Mader.

- Be relentless
"If at first you don't succeed, try, try again." If I had given up on my dream of achieving success in the United States, I never would have gotten out of Illinois. If Mader had backed down from his argument in the hall with his top client, he might have lost the deal. If Elon Musk had given up on his dream to run an Internet-based financial company, X.com never would have become PayPal. It simply would have been another casualty of the tech bubble's bursting.

Adventure comes with its share of adversity. You are bound—no, *certain* to face a few setbacks. If it were easy to be an entrepreneur, then everyone would have a startup. Everyone would be rich. So get the word out, set goals for yourself, and, by all means, never give up.

New American Philosophy: For a Greater Sense of Adventure, Surround Yourself with Risk Takers

According to Ric Fulop of Northbridge Venture Partners, a huge part of being a successful entrepreneur is leaning on your adventurousness and ignoring the risks inherent in the business process.

"Startups are very delicate organisms," he revealed. "There is always a lot of risk in what you're doing. Until you're profitable and cash-flow positive, there is always risk."

According to Fulop, the risk is what makes the project worth doing. If you aren't willing to embark on the occasional adventure, you shouldn't be an entrepreneur in the first place.

Another important lesson to gather from this remarkable entrepreneur is that the adventure needs to be constant.

"Even when your startup is up and running, you're competing against a lot of folks with more money and resources than you," he said in our interview. The moment you lose that spirit of adventure and competition is the moment your startup will begin to flounder. The solution? "You have to surround yourself with good people who can help you develop technology that gives you a competitive edge."

In business and in life, if you're not doing something that excites you, you're wasting your time. New American Millionaires succeed because they're willing to follow their senses of adventure into the unknown. Entrepreneurs are adventurous by nature—and the most adventurous among them are often the most likely to reach millionaire status. If you have an idea for how to improve your life, pursue it. Failure in pursuit of a dream is far easier to live with than failure as a result of not pursuing a dream. If you hope to become like the New American Millionaires, you cannot let your doubts prevent you from taking flight.

In this chapter you learned the value of getting out there and meeting new people. You were exposed to the value of setting lofty goals and pursuing them relentlessly. You have seen the value of taking action for action's sake. Thanks to Ric Fulop, you know an adventurous spirit often benefits from being among risk-takers.

When pursuing your entrepreneurial goals, if you find yourself retreating into your fears, often the best remedy is to seek the advice or aid of the most adventurous businesspeople you know. Always remember every successful entrepreneur alive today had to be adventurous at one point or another. You don't reach the top without a willingness to take a few risks and brave the often rocky path to success.

Keep the lessons of this chapter in mind as you begin to nurture your own sense of adventure. When you're feeling brave enough to pursue even your wildest dreams, you will be ready to move on to the next trait in the New American Millionaire model. In the chapter to come, you will learn how to identify resources where most people would see only deficits. When you have gained that ability, you will know how to make something of nothing and how to stretch your time, money, and skills further than the competition.

Chapter 8

Resourceful: How to Become Your Own Personal Rainmaker

To be thrown upon one's own resources is to be cast into the very lap of fortune; for our faculties then undergo a development and display an energy of which they were previously unsusceptible.
—**Benjamin Franklin**

I LOVE THIS QUOTE. It is, at its core, a reminder that the darkest of times actually can benefit those who are able to find rays of light in the darkness. In America, from an economic perspective, there have been few times darker than the present. But from out of this turmoil, a new wave of entrepreneurs and innovators will be born. Whether you are among them will depend on your ability to get creative, and to determine ways to meet needs and make money in an environment where money is scarce.

This chapter is about resourcefulness, the ability to overcome and make ends meet in an otherwise difficult situation. Those who are able to overcome, both New Americans and millionaires alike, do so because they see advantages in their lives where others see only despair. While the masses quiver in fear of a crippling recession, the resourceful look to the people, talents, and circumstances that give them an edge over the competition and allow them to flourish in an otherwise less than ideal situation. It isn't always about figuring out how to do more with less either. It's about adapting your talents to meet new and previously unforeseen needs. It's about reaching out to the people who may be in positions to help you. And it's about shaping the resources you have so they're better in line to propel you toward your ultimate goal.

During my adjustment to life in America, resourcefulness proved essential. My first months in California were relatively fun. I reunited with my aunt, made a few friends, and enjoyed the business of looking for a job. It was summer when I arrived, so I knew I would need to get a job as quickly as possible so I could earn enough money to help pay for the upcoming fall semester at university. In time I secured a job with Barclays Bank of California courtesy of my father, who had served that bank for more than twenty-five years as an area manager in my country. I was a summer intern and drew budget graphs for eight hours every day. At the time I felt privileged, as this was a "clean" job where I dressed up like a budding executive and sat at my own desk. But at the end of summer, the bank terminated my contract and I was left to fend for myself.

A month into the fall semester, I began to feel the pangs of financial pressure. The money I had earned depleted rapidly, leaving me uncertain as to whether I would be able to meet the cost of attending school. There were times when funds were so scarce I didn't even know when my next meal would be. So I threw myself into my studies. I would come home to my dilapidated studio apartment on the outskirts of San Francisco every night and pore over my books and homework. In time my routine boiled down to school during the day, homework whenever I could manage it, and job hunting in the evening.

Eventually I found work through the university, but it was degrading labor. I went from a suit, tie, and desk job in the summer to the inglorious life of cleaning toilets in the fall. The pay was meager— not nearly enough to defray my tuition and rent. But despite my budget shortfalls, I continued to persevere.

In the third month, when I couldn't pay my rent, my landlord evicted me. For the first time in my life, I was truly homeless. In circumstances such as these, the resourceful would turn to their friends. I did have friends, but at the time I didn't feel like I had known them long enough to burden them with my dirty laundry (literally and figuratively).

But the resourceful are always tough. My tough alternative was to park my car at whatever location seemed safest and spend my nights in the cramped backseat. I kept myself clean and presentable by committing to a carefully scheduled rotation with friends, wherein I would visit a friend's home, pretend to be late for work, and request to use their shower. My friends would always agree, but I never felt comfortable asking for this favor more than once in a given week. So I would rotate from one friend to the next, repeating the cycle only when it became absolutely necessary.

Those days of living in my car represented the closest I have ever come to giving up and surrendering myself to the immigration department for deportation. The winter cold was biting. My passion overwhelmed me. Fear of the unknown and of being terrorized by anyone who might have stumbled across my car dominated my mind. I began to accept the idea that I had failed myself and my family. On many nights I thought of death as a sweet release. I felt dejected and helpless; I was a man living in a situation my culture would have considered shameful. I had come seeking a new life, hoping to gain access to a better education and the potential for a high-paying job, and here I found myself cleaning toilets and living in my car.

In time my determination to succeed in this country won over my feelings of despair. I pooled what little resources I had, relied on my friends for help and food, and began looking anew for work.

Sometimes being resourceful is a matter of knowing the right people. Sometimes it's a matter of networking to help alleviate an existing problem. Sometimes it's building alliances to help you achieve a future outcome. And sometimes, as David Yahid, founder and CEO of Couture Designer European Clothing, San Francisco, pointed out, resourcefulness is simply a matter of the right things falling into place at the right time.

Yahid's moment of greatest need came on the day he learned the building in which he had housed his company for ten years would be repurposed for another business venture. The landlord had sold it to another owner who envisioned different things for the building. He wanted to develop it into condos and ride the wave of the real estate market at the time.

For Yahid this was particularly devastating because the building in question had been the literal house for his brand. He had spent a decade using this storefront to generate recognition in the community. By then a great deal of his business depended on local and repeat customers. If he were forced to move, he would be forced to take a step backward in the evolution of his business.

As Yahid suggested, it is often best in circumstances like these to turn to the experts in your inner circle. While he knew very little about contract law, he did have people he could trust to teach him about the rigors of his lease.

"You have to surround yourself with knowledgeable people," Yahid revealed. "In circumstances like these, they can be invaluable."

As I've mentioned, luck can often play a part in resourcefulness. Yahid leveraged every knowledge base, colleague, and mentor he could to help save his storefront. He met with the new landlord to try to hammer out a deal for his store to remain. But, in the end, what prevented him from having to move was a downturn in the real estate market. With the wavering economy, the new landlord began to think maintaining the building as-is would be a more prudent business move than trying to flip it into something new.

Success as a New American requires help and oftentimes a little luck. The same can be said for entrepreneurs. In neither case will the person succeed unless he is willing to take advantage of those areas where he is lucky or has access to people and resources where others do not. Many people fail in their business pursuits simply because they fail to recognize the many advantages they possess. Of those who do recognize them, many simply do not know how or do not wish to exploit them. Fortunately it is possible to learn how to identify the resources in your life. And once you have those resources in mind, you can learn the steps necessary to put them to work for you.

Consider first the following tips on how to recognize your advantages:

- Assess the situation

  Every entrepreneur, however successful, faces difficult times. When such a problem arises, the most important thing is not to dwell on the problem itself. Many faced with financial shortfalls, for instance, would simply allow thoughts of money shortages to live as dark clouds over all their business decisions. If you make decisions with money foremost in your mind, those decisions aren't always beneficial. The best course of action is to take the time to assess the problem. Define what it means in the present, what it means for your business, and what it is likely to mean in the future. You will never be able to move past the problem until you can clearly define its severity and nature.

  Begin by asking yourself what it would take to overcome the problem given ideal circumstances.

  "Do not put any constraints on yourself," Gupta advises. "Ask yourself, if you could raise an infinite amount of money or recruit anyone you wanted, what would it take—and what would you do—to get the ship straight?"

  Answering questions like these allows you to see from a distance exactly how much you might need to make this problem an easy one to resolve. Once you know the peak of what you need, you can begin figuring out resourceful ways to get by with less. Find more questions like these in the resources questionnaire at **www.milliondollarsuccessinstitute.com**.

- Measure your exterior resources

  With the definition of your problem in place, you may now begin the process of determining solutions. But let's not skip a step here. Solutions will come in time, but you will not arrive at the proper solutions unless you take the time to assess the advantages you have at your disposal. For the truly resourceful, advantages come in two forms: exterior resources (like money, business contacts, and assets) and interior resources (like creativity, determination, and fearlessness). Most tend to dwell on the exterior resources, so let's begin with those.

First off, as every entrepreneur will tell you, it is incredibly easy to fall into the trap of thinking your business is only as healthy as the amount of money it has at its disposal. As Jerry Yang of Yahoo! pointed out, money is only a small percentage of the battle: "The challenge for us is to build partnerships over time that will realize the benefits others are gaining through mergers and acquisitions," he said. The point here is that when measured against the funding and power of mega-conglomerations, there is nothing quite like a valuable partnership to drive a business to the top. You may find your competition is larger and better funded than you, but if you seek valuable partnerships with smart and capable people and companies, you will find yourself becoming something quite a bit more powerful than the underdog. You will have the independence, the resources, and the mind power to go toe to toe even with the largest corporations in your field.

So when you are faced with a particular challenge in your market, start by creating a list of the people in your life. List everyone. It doesn't matter whether you think at the moment they can help you professionally; every person in your life has the potential to help you. Some can offer financial support. Others make nice sounding boards for ideas and brainstorming. Still others can offer their time, energy, or emotional support.

Beyond these people, there are, of course, the professionals you know. Sometimes they can help with matters that require special knowledge (like law, finance, or marketing). Finally, don't forget to add total strangers to your list. If you know someone who might be in position to help you professionally, don't be afraid to list him simply because you haven't yet introduced yourself. Every person who stands the chance to help you belongs on this list. And if you haven't met everyone on your final list yet, your first task is to start reaching out to the strangers.

Next assess the information available to you. Information is incredibly valuable. If you are aware of a demand shortfall in the marketplace, that can help you. If you are aware of something your competition isn't providing to its customers, that can help you. Even information you do not yet have belongs on this list. If you have yet to determine the full financials on a new concept, write that down and then work toward bridging the gap. Visit the library. Call an expert. Research, research, research.

The third list is often the only one that entrepreneurs pay any attention to—and that almost always leads to their downfall. This list has to do with money, which does in fact rule everything. However, although it maintains a firm grip on the things we can and can't do, that grip is not infallible. The first step is to assess what income you can count on, what income you can expect to be less reliable, and what expenses you can expect to meet. In times of surplus, be sure to save. In times of deficit, don't let that overwhelming feeling of shortfall get the best of you. Being resourceful means pinching every penny. If you don't have enough money, try a fundraiser. Reach out to friends and family who are in positions to help you. Seek out a venture capitalist. Visit the bank and ask for a loan. And, when all else fails, consider searching for a second job.

The same goes for assets. Most entrepreneurs don't realize the assets they have at their disposal. While I would never recommend sleeping in your car, a means of transportation at your disposal can be a useful tool when it comes to improving business prospects. Consider each object you own and then determine ways to use it to your advantage. If there is something you need—like a computer, for example—and you don't have enough money for it, consider creative ways of getting hold of one cheaper. Reach out to colleagues; inquire with businesses; borrow from loved ones. Assets, whatever their condition, always hold value. The truly resourceful determine ways to acquire more assets for less while getting more from the assets they already have at hand.

• Measure your inherent resources
When considering the advantages available to you, it is easy to dwell on the exterior. Too many entrepreneurs base their outlooks solely on the money, people, and assets at their disposal. They will give up on a concept because they have failed to garner any venture capital or business loans. When a particularly important contact rebuffs their attempts to connect, they assume it means their idea wasn't good enough. Some look at their mortgaged homes, their leased cars, and their meager incomes and assume these things are somehow innovation-prohibitive.

The resourceful remember that exterior resources are only half the picture. Regardless of their financial or social situations, the resourceful are able to rely on their creativity, intelligence, confidence, courage, discipline, passion, and skill to make the impossible possible. While the competition is busy fretting about how they will ever get their businesses off the ground, the resourceful are out making it happen. They have a better understanding of the value they bring to the table, and they don't let the stressors of the outside world getting in their way.

When considering your own resources, do not forget to include your inherent value. You might not have the money or the connections, but you do have the skills that will allow you to gain both in time. If you are passionate about your idea and willing to put in the hard work, you will succeed in the end. In America passion and brilliance always win.

The other nice thing about inherent resources is they don't diminish if you don't let them. Money runs out. People change allegiances. Assets lose their value. But the more you use your creativity, the more creative you become. The more you boost your own confidence, the more it helps you meet your goals. The more courageous you are, the more obstacles you overcome. And the more obstacles you overcome, the more your courage builds.

The point here is that inherent resources are under your control. No matter what happens, assuming you put in the effort, they will never lose value. And the more powerful your inherent resources are, the more likely they are to lead to exterior resources like wealth and security. With that in mind, it would behoove you to value them above all things.

You now have a series of lists that demonstrate your many advantages. With those lists in hand, the picture doesn't look quite so bleak, does it? Always remember that even in the darkest of times, these rays of hope are available to you. Money might decline, assets might depreciate, but your intellect and your creativity will never die. With that in mind, let us move now to a method of using your advantages to better your entrepreneurial situation.

- Choose your weapons
  Thanks to your lists, you know exactly what resources you have available to you. The best way to begin putting those resources to work is to determine which of them apply to your particular problem. Not all of your business contacts will be able to help you. Not all of your skills will apply. Check your lists and mark off which will be most valuable in the hunt for what you need.

- Brainstorm
  Far too often even the most creative entrepreneurs get stuck on one track of thinking. It can be an easy thing to assume that what has worked for you in the past will work again in the future. But if you find the outcome appears to be different this time, the worst thing you can do is approach the problem in the same way you always have. Einstein once said the definition of insanity is to try the same thing twice and expect different results. So get creative. Don't be afraid to try new approaches. Even if your ideas seem crazy, you won't know their viability

until you put them into action. If you find yourself faced with a negative outcome, sit down, brainstorm, and put together as many new approaches as possible—however ludicrous or unconventional they might seem.

- Test and retest
  So you find yourself faced with a particularly troubling problem. You've sat down and brainstormed potential solutions. The next logical step is to put your solutions to the test. Don't be afraid to try these new approaches even if they don't seem like they will work. A willingness to take risks is a huge part of what separates successful entrepreneurs from the unsuccessful. Experimenting with new ideas is the essence of risk taking. Remember that because these ideas are new, they might require a more concerted effort on your part—and they may require adaptation along the way. But by all means try everything you can think of. You might be surprised by what you learn simply by trying.

- Apply Band-Aids
  It's easy to get stuck in the mindset that you're never going to overcome your problem unless you come up with a long-term solution. Cash-flow problems, for example, are always best met with a permanent increase in revenue. But permanent increases in revenue are rarely easy to come by. Maybe you're waiting for a particularly big prospect to become a client, infusing your business with the perfect amount of cash to get yourself back on the right track. If that's the case, what happens if that prospect keeps waffling or putting off payment? Your business would be left with an open wound in terms of cash flow.

  Sometimes meeting that long-term solution requires a few short-term fixes. For cash flow, consider taking out a bank loan or leaning on your friends, family, and business contacts. It's not an ideal situation, but Band-Aids such as these can go a long way. They help to heal the inevitable scrapes and bruises of entrepreneurship. Without them no good business could hope to survive.

- Jump at every opportunity
  Sometimes we get so caught up in our problems we start to suffer from tunnel vision. Nothing else in business or in life makes sense until we can figure out how to overcome our problem. When this happens it becomes easier to miss opportunities we otherwise might have embraced with open arms. Don't lose the forest for the trees. A good entrepreneur always keeps an open mind and an open set of eyes. He always looks out for that next opportunity, and when it presents itself he is quick to jump on it. So don't let your problems become distractions. Seek opportunities. Be decisive. And follow whatever path out of the dark you can find.

New American Philosophy: Sometimes You *Have* to Jump

Dame DC Cordova, CEO of Excellerated Business Schools, recalls a time when she was forced literally to pick up everything she had accomplished in her business and move it to another continent. In the late 1990s, her primary business avenues had been opened up in the Asia Pacific region, but by late '97 and early '98, the regional economy had begun to stagnate. Where her business had recently been booming in Singapore, there now seemed little hope of expansion. In many ways it looked like it could be the end for Cordova's company.

But the resourceful never give up. They assess the problem and work on ways to make it their solution. Using the lessons of her business schools, Cordova packed up and moved from her home office in Hawaii to San Diego, California. In many ways this was like starting from square one for Cordova. She had spent so many years in the Asia Pacific region learning from mentors, picking up the basics, and building an organization, and she now had to complete these tasks again.

"As we teach in our business school," she explained, "If you want to succeed in a new market, you have to master three key areas: sales and marketing, people and organizations, and money and finances." When Cordova first arrived in San Diego, she had her sales technique and her desirable product already in hand, but she knew very few people, and she was in debt financially. To overcome the latter two needs, she had to get resourceful. She had to network like never before. And in the absence of money, she had to build relationships with potential alliance partners based on trust and a mutual understanding that work would be performed under the promise of future profits.

Taking a leap like this can be a trying thing, and it is certainly adventurous. But as Cordova has pointed out, the resourceful can survive just about anything as long as they have the right tools, the right product, and the right people around them. It also helps to have patience. It took Cordova eighteen months to establish her business in a new country. But thanks to that patience and that resourcefulness, her company thrives today.

On the topic of resourcefulness, I would like to offer this simple reminder: never give up. How many successful businesses would have failed had their enterprising founders thrown in the towel at the first sign of trouble? Few good businesses rise to the top without taking a few lumps along the way. Just as is the case with New Americans, only those entrepreneurs who are willing to stare down adversity, innovate, and overcome realize the greatest success.

In this chapter you have learned how to assess your unique business situation, measure your interior and exterior resources, and then formulate a plan for overcoming your obstacles by carefully mixing and matching the most appropriate resources for the task. Remember, sometimes solutions require a little brainstorming, and they certainly require some trial and error. Don't be afraid to hold back and ponder potential solutions from time to time. That said, don't be afraid to act when it's appropriate either. If that means settling for short-term fixes, then so be it. You must do whatever it takes to succeed. In the end remember that even failures have their lessons, and, as DC Cordova teaches us, the best entrepreneurs recognize that all failures can be opportunities in disguise.

When you have fully absorbed and incorporated the messages that comprise this trait, you will be ready to move on to the next component of the New American Millionaire model. In the chapter to come, you will learn the tips and tricks for becoming more innovative—a valuable lesson, as innovation is often the central driving force behind small-business growth.

Chapter 9

Innovative: You are the Next Big Thing; You Just Don't Know it Yet

Imagination is more important than knowledge.
—Albert Einstein

PETER DRUCKER, ONE OF the true gurus of management theory (and himself an immigrant), once said, "Innovation is the specific instrument of entrepreneurship. It is the act that endows resources with a new capacity to create wealth." In other words all advancement in terms of business and wealth is derived from innovation. It is the reason for change and progression. It has launched a million businesses and created a million millionaires.

For Jerry Yang of Yahoo!, in this current entrepreneurial landscape, innovation is greater capital even than money. "I think that it's always possible to have a great company if you have great ideas," he said. "I will say that since the web has become more commercialized, it also takes some good financial resources to build a great business, but as I always

100

say, you have to have the idea first." So it doesn't matter what condition you find your funding in if you do not first have a great idea to propel your business forward. For these reasons we would do well in our study to examine exactly what it takes to develop an innovative spirit.

At its core business innovation is a matter of realizing opportunity in an unmet demand in the marketplace. Truly innovative entrepreneurs are able to see opportunities where others see only competition. They can look out across the masses and identify something they are not yet receiving—a need that is not yet met by existing companies or entrepreneurs. And once they've identified that need, they're able to develop cost-effective and attractive ways to meet it.

In many ways the New American Millionaire has this kind of innovation built in. But where the entrepreneur must spot demand in the marketplace, for the New American Millionaire the demand often hits closer to home. The demand I speak of in this case is a mere matter of survival. For me the act of living in my car while I collected sparse wages created a demand for more money, a better job, and the need to change my outlook on what I could and could not afford. It was a matter of thinking outside the box, of changing my perspective about what mattered most to me in life and what it would take to get it.

During my third year of college I reached a breaking point that required a new brand of thinking. By then I'd had it with menial jobs. My humiliation over having to latch on to friends for help (that they sometimes didn't even know they were giving) had come to a boil. Quite frankly I had grown furious with the whole system for not being fairer to a poor international student.

My first step was to revise my dreams. Where I had originally dreamt of gaining a high-level American education and then going on to secure a stable and high-paying American job, I now dreamt only of the day when I would finally be freed from the bonds of dependence. I knew my education would make me marketable to future employers, but I also knew I couldn't take another day of scrubbing toilets. I simply wanted more for myself.

I came to the painful realization that the environment I found myself in would no longer do for my dreams. I would one day need an education, certainly, but if I was going to get it I would have to turn my envisioned path on its head. I would have to innovate a new path for myself, a new way of obtaining all the things I wanted in my New American life. So I decided that after completing my third year of college, I would begin looking for a decent job—one that would allow me to work in an office and would pay a reasonable wage.

In time that opportunity came to me in the form of a sales career. On the advice of my friend, Amos, I accepted an offer to work as a captive agent for Allstate Insurance Company. The job would be difficult, given that it required long hours, cold calling, and its fair share of stress brought about by compulsory performance quotas. But it would represent the beginning of my path to financial success. It would be the point where I would begin my journey from New American to New American Millionaire.

At first I did everything by the book. I stumbled over the many new competencies I needed to learn. When calling customers and prospects, my approach over the phone was clumsy—particularly considering that my accent back then was thicker than it is now. Meanwhile my face-to-face meetings with clients left me feeling hollow because I never seemed to connect in the way the standards and practices of the company seemed to indicate. My manager kept the pressure on me, kept driving me to reach more customers and make more sales. In many ways he pushed me to the brink of my breaking point.

It would take me a few months to realize that if I hoped to succeed, I would need something more than what I could find in the sales manuals. I would need to innovate. I would need to do something other agents weren't doing—something that would help me stand out from the competition in such a way as to overcome my initial shortcomings as a salesman. For me that innovation came in the form of audio and video business cards. Indeed I was the first in the company to devise such a strategy. In the hopes of breaking the ice, delivering my message, and connecting with the prospect or client prior to any face-to-face meetings, I would create audio and video messages that could be distributed via DVD or jump drive. In the messages I would educate the client or prospect on the value of my company and its products, offer testimonials from my satisfied clients, and provide a brief summary of my credentials.

In short order I discovered this new approach would change everything for me. I would give these audio/video business cards to anyone who would take them. And it quickly became clear the messages softened the prospects and warm them up to me and my presentation. By the time we would finally meet, it would be as if they already knew and trusted me. They had seen my face or heard my voice in a prerecorded message after all.

Using these audio/video business cards led directly to an eighty-percent increase in my sales figures. The results were nothing short of astounding. I went from struggling just to make calls to struggling to keep up with the calls that were coming in. It was a remarkable change—and certainly a positive one—but I wasn't about to rest on my laurels. The truly innovative never stop innovating. So I took my success and rolled it into a seminar program. On a regular basis, I would set up events and invite all my prospective clients to attend. The prospects who came to my workshops would get to experience my knowledge of the products, sample my natural empathy toward their situations, and, in the end, often wind up making appointments to further discuss their options with me.

So there I was with my audio/video business cards (a powerful tool to help me knock on my prospects' doors), my seminar programs (a powerful tool to help me get my prospects to open the doors), and the resultant face-to-face meetings (where I would then have the opportunity to close the deal). I had realized a deficit in my ability to reach strangers and sell them on a product and had innovated a method to help me overcome that deficit. My newness to the sales process and my newness to the country and its culture no longer mattered. I could now begin the journey to my dream.

To pack up and leave one's country requires the ability to see a brighter future for oneself. To make it as an immigrant in the United States, the New American Millionaire must have the ability to think in ways others do not. He must be able to overcome obstacles with new and innovative solutions. The desire to create a profitable company has its root in these same values. One must be able to see a demand where others do not—and, more importantly, predict the best ways to meet that demand in an attractive and affordable way. Innovative entrepreneurs must be able to make connections where they never existed before. They must be willing and able to surround themselves with a diverse set of people, ideas, and perspectives. They must be ready to accept a little trial and error. They must always question the norms and work on ways to circumvent them. And, above all, they must be able to observe and identify the needs and wants of a broad range of people.

All of this might sound difficult, but it is indeed possible to absorb all those valuable tendencies listed above. The old wisdom is that some people are born creative while others are not. But studies have shown that while innovation is indeed an inherent trait, the skills that make one person more innovative than the next can be learned. Some people might be born with the propensity to innovate, but creativity is, in the main, an acquired trait. In other words anyone can learn to be innovative. They simply need to adapt to and follow these steps.

How to Create like a New American Millionaire

Innovation is about the spirit of creation—that drive to see the way the world or a particular business, product, or service operates and then determine how to make it operate in a better or more efficient way. It's about seeing the potential in something and making that potential a reality. It doesn't take just creativity but a certain kind of grit and determination that few people possess, but many can learn. Innovation is often the only thing that separates a good company from an unsuccessful one. It is what allows the enterprising entrepreneur to keep his company afloat in the dark times and keep it fresh and ever-evolving even when things are going well.

Innovation is what makes Silicon Valley such a wonderful place to live, work, and establish a startup business. There are many reasons for this, and they all contribute directly to *how* to innovate most effectively. When I asked the entrepreneurs I interviewed for this book about what it takes to be innovative in America, almost all of them cited Silicon Valley. So, with that in mind, let's consider a few steps toward innovation that can be observed or overheard in just about any coffee shop in the region.

- Ask yourself, "What is being done right now?"
  The first and most logical step toward any innovative purpose is to research and consider everything you know about the company, industry, product or service, or market need you hope to create or evolve. It's impossible to know what people want (or even all those things they don't know they want yet) if you don't have a clue as to the current state of affairs. There could be a company out there that does something similar to what you want to do and you believe that you can do it better.

  Often, performing diligent market research is the difference between *knowing* whether there is a need and simply *perceiving* it. Establishing a formal process for market research will help you to learn exactly what the industry or market lacks, which will in turn allow you to determine ways to meet those challenges. The process typically leads to the revelation of areas where you might be able to develop an innovative advantage over the competition as well. Even once your startup is up and running, market research is a key process to lean upon. Companies that get complacent with their existing innovations and market knowledge often wind up careening toward irrelevance.

  "I love to study the other players in the industry," said Gabriel Nossovitch, cofounder of WorldWorks Inc. in the US along with many other personal transformation companies throughout Latin America. His organizations offer transformational seminars dedicated to personal growth. They also attempt to raise awareness in underprivileged populations through large-scale community-service projects staged throughout the Americas. "I explore and experiment. Any company that is of a similar nature, I will go and watch what they are doing so I can figure out how they do it and how I might do it better."

  Oftentimes, when assessing the market needs and competition, it is a good thing to be as much insider as outsider.

You can't accurately assess public and corporate needs unless you're plugged in to the people who know. Surrounding yourself with an intricate network of subject-matter experts is often a good practice. Observe, listen, and ask questions of these people. The answers they provide will often unlock new avenues to innovation.

New American Philsophy: Listen to Your Intuition

According to Rajan Raghavan, cofounder of companies like Ankeena, Xambala, RealChip Communications, and Virtual Chips, market research only takes you so far. "You have to listen to both the market and your intuition," he said in our interview. In Raghavan's model intuition is the number one influence on innovation. Market research is secondary. "You have to have a formal process for market research," he revealed, "but market research isn't what got my companies going. What got me going was intuition. Market research is just a way to validate that intuition."

This is an interesting point to consider. It means that a substantial part of being a successful entrepreneur is the ability to follow your feelings on a given matter. You can't do this without fearlessness. You can't simply act on a whim if you don't have the guts and passion to believe in your ideas and make them a reality. If you can bring yourself to the point where you believe your intuition is valid, and you do not allow your fear of failure to disrupt that belief, then your intuition will carry you further than market research ever could.

- Ask yourself, "How can I do it better?"
  Now that you're aware of what the market needs, you can begin to examine how you are the only person in the world who can meet those needs. And you are. Remember that point. There is no one else on the planet with your unique skillset. If you feel you have found a new niche or a new innovation to exploit, there is no one else who can address those points quite like

you can. Sure, there are other people who can meet these same needs, but not in the same way. You bring things to the table they cannot.

So now it is time to turn the examination inward. Assess your skills. Assess your perceived opportunities and advantages. Assess your contacts. Consider how the latest technology might be employed to help make a given process, product, or service run more smoothly and efficiently. Then put that information to work.

Often, in today's rapidly evolving business world, technology is the answer to innovation. "I love to try to match technology with my vision," said Nossovitch. "I often find that any innovation can be enhanced with the latest technology. In my own companies, if we can use emerging technologies to help raise awareness, we never hesitate."

- Diversify
  A large majority of the entrepreneurs I interviewed for this book expressed thankfulness for having surrounded themselves with people from many different cultural, ethnic, and educational backgrounds. Two minds are better than one. Three are better than two. And it is of special benefit to innovation if those three minds are as different from one another as possible. Nossovitch's company wouldn't be where it is today without its network of trainers from all over the world—or his vision to mix and match those backgrounds in many different settings across the globe. Often, when there is a perceived problem in business, it is the collective, and not the brilliant individual, that discovers the best way to overcome that problem.

  The same can be said for a setting. If you find yourself going into the same conference room every day, meeting with the same people about the same problems and coming up with the same tired solutions, then the answer might be a matter of just changing the scenery. Get out of the building. Change rooms. Involve new people. Involve more people. Involve less people—whatever it takes to break the mold of how you have been working to date. There is no inspiration in the same old same old.

New American Philosphy: Noodle Night

Henry Wong, CEO of Diamond TechVentures and a prolific entrepreneur with a 25-year history of success in Silicon Valley, learned early on that getting people out of their established work-environment comfort zones often leads to great opportunities for innovation.

"The interesting thing we started when I was with XaQti Semiconductor," Wong revealed, "is that we had these diverse cultural backgrounds. We discovered early on that these backgrounds worked well and humbly together, but that they would often lead to the best creativity if we changed the environment from time to time."

Wong's solution? "Every Wednesday night we would have a noodle night. We would all meet for an evening meal of noodles. It seems trivial, but having a meeting in a less-corporate and structured setting would allow people to speak more openly about how we could improve the company."

Surrounding yourself with a diverse set of minds only goes so far if those minds remain closed off by the rigors of work etiquette. Very few people are the same at the office as they are at home. There is a certain amount of dynamism that is lost when we construct the walls we all construct around our working personalities. Bringing a little of our home lives into the working environment often allows people to set aside those walls and assert themselves in new and more open ways.

"Remember," Wong said, "Wednesday night is noodle night."

- Be willing to take the chance
  Innovation isn't always a matter of seeing something no one else has seen yet. GM wasn't the first to market the automobile,

but they are the largest car manufacturer in the US today. What separates the successful innovators from the dreamers is always that willingness to take the chance. Those who simply dream never see their ideas become realities. Those who innovate are always quick to act.

It doesn't matter how much research you do, how many inspired and creative people you surround yourself with, or how detailed you make your plan for innovation; if you don't have the courage and conviction to act on your idea it will never get off the ground. So follow your passion. Believe in your ideas and your abilities. Take the steps to make your innovations realities. If they fail, so be it. Go back to the drawing board and revise. If they succeed, don't rest on your laurels. The companies that survive long-term—the companies that remain on the path to unstoppable riches—are those that never stop innovating.

You have what it takes to innovate. Everyone does. You are observant. If you can motivate yourself properly, you can do the research necessary to discover avenues for innovation. You know people who can help you brainstorm or otherwise make your dreams realities—and if you don't then you are capable of building your professional network. You have put in the time and developed an idea. Now is when the real work begins. Get out there and make your idea happen. Follow your plan, lean on your network and research, and become the next successful entrepreneur.

In this chapter you have gained insight into all the components that make for brilliant innovation. When you're ready to follow your intuition for improving existing processes or products, you will find yourself in a position to hone and refine your insight and your craft. In the next chapter, you will see just how valuable such focus can be to the New American Millionaire.

Chapter 10

Focused: Distractions Prevent Wealth. Period.

Concentrate all your thoughts upon the work at hand.
The sun's rays do not burn until brought to focus.
—Alexander Graham Bell

THE LIFE OF THE entrepreneur is one of many potential distractions. Running a successful business requires attention to detail on a wide range of critically important elements. Often, once a business is up and running, the primary attribute that separates the successful entrepreneur from those whose businesses fold is an ability to focus on all the most important tasks at hand. Those who can properly block out distractions and get their jobs done find themselves in far better positions to succeed.

For me, finding that necessary focus did not come until after I saw that initial success in my financial services career. Once I realized I was able to make sales, two things happened. First I gained the confidence that I could do this—meaning I knew I had the attributes necessary for getting the job done. I had the determination, the big dreams, the ability, and the willingness to work long hours, and my fear of rejection dissipated. Second I knew that since I had completed the process of making a sale once, I could repeat that process and enjoy the same success. I knew with consistent and focused repetitive effort, my results could be scaled to larger profits and, ultimately, unlimited success.

And that's the key term for this chapter: focus. It's the ability to block out all distractions and concentrate on only those things that are most important to achieving something. In my sales career, before I found my focus, the distractions that got the best of me included those bad habits that often come when a person who has suffered through poverty finally finds himself earning consistent money. In short I overindulged, living the high-roller life of expensive vacations and big, fast cars. This led to a quick dissipation in the money I had earned, and before I knew it I was clawing to make more sales so I could keep up again.

It was then that I learned to focus—I learned that I would always need to remember where I came from and where I was going. I would need to stop concentrating on the quick pleasures of sudden wealth and return my focus to the job at hand. Without that focus, all my hard work would be burned up by negative energy. I hadn't made it yet, though I had briefly believed it so. No, if I wanted to enjoy serious long-term success, I would need to stick to concentrating on all the lessons I had learned in the pursuit of my dreams.

As soon as I became more focused, my attitude coalesced into something greater than before. Where I had approached my early sales with a kind of desperation, I now decided I would maintain a cheerful, outgoing attitude in all business operations. This seemed to draw people to me. My sphere of influence grew simply because I focused my energies on helping others to feel good about themselves.

New American Millionaires seem to be more prepared to focus on personal and career success compared to their host-country counterparts. They appear to possess restless energy and self-discipline almost from the moment they land in this country. Perhaps this is the result of the magic of America itself—that promise of a land filled with visible and attainable opportunity. Or perhaps it is derived from the razor-keen sense of determination that seems so ingrained in the immigrant spirit. Whatever the case, focus and determination are significant parts of the entrepreneurial recipe for success. For many New American Millionaires these attributes are imbued by culture, upbringing, and circumstance. But for others focus is an attribute that can be learned.

How to Achieve Focus

There is nothing deadlier to an entrepreneurial career than a lack of focus. If you're trying to do too much or if you get too caught up in the negativity of something that isn't going quite right, it can lead to missed assignments, shortfalls in work ethic, or, worst of all, indecision. Every successful business is defined by the abilities of its leader, and a good leader cannot allow a lack of focus to derail his work. For this reason one of the key elements of realizing success similar to that of the New American Millionaires is to work on ways to improve your focus. In this effort consider the following tips:

- Bring your goals to the center

  No one gets anywhere without specific goals in mind. So why is it that so many would-be entrepreneurs tend to set goals and then forget about them? There is nothing more detrimental to focus than losing sight of your initial goals. Just like New American Millionaire who struggles in his first months in America, you must remember the reason you decided to embark upon this adventure in the first place. If you forget why you're here, you are likely to be overwhelmed by the negativity and distraction of the frequent setbacks in business and in life.

  It's likely that by now you have established what your goals are. It's possible you've even written them down. Perhaps they're part of your company's mission statement or business plan. But until you start living by those goals and concentrating all your efforts on achieving them, they are little more than words on paper.

  If you find yourself having trouble maintaining focus on your work, it's time to revisit your established goals. Study them, reimagine them, reinvigorate or even revise them if need be. Often a quick review of your preliminary goals is all you will need to block out the things that have come to sow the seeds of doubt. Once you've done this, you may return to your dilemma with a renewed sense of where you're heading. You can begin by envisioning the end result. See yourself achieving your goals. What does that reality look like? What would you give to reach that reality? What do you need to get there? With the answers to these questions in mind, you will be in better position to create a more detailed plan of attack for overcoming your obstacles and distractions and getting back on the path to success.

- Work on ways to eliminate distraction
  It might seem simple, but oftentimes the biggest detriments to focus are the little things that stand closest to us on a daily basis. If you have an important deadline to meet or a key decision to make, your cluttered desk and the blaring television and the noise from the hallway are not helping you. Clean up and lock down.

  The same goes for the clutter on your computer. First, don't spend time on programs or websites that distract you from your work. Second, don't let your e-mails overwhelm you. Remember, no successful entrepreneur can be expected to answer every single e-mail he receives every day. By the time you get to the point where you're managing a major company, those daily e-mails will number in the hundreds. So start practicing the fine art of filtering out all the communications of lesser importance. Focus only on that which matters now, in this moment.

  Speaking of which, manage your moments carefully. Plan your days from start to finish. If you know exactly what you need to be doing and when, it goes a long way toward freeing your mind for the important things like making decisions and being productive on your short- and long-term goals. If you find it's easy for you to become distracted from the tasks at hand, stick to your schedule religiously. Rather than answering the phone every time it rings, schedule time during the day to dedicate specifically to returning phone calls. Just let it ring and go to voicemail. And when the part of your day designated for calls comes, get down to returning those voicemails.

For more information visit **www.milliondollarsuccessinstitute.com**. There you will find a link to a pair of tools to help you identify and eliminate distractions as well as plan your day to the fullest.

- Celebrate successes, learn from defeats

  Those who get hung up on negative results—or even the minor imperfections of the things they achieve—tend to perform at much lower levels than those who are more willing and able to celebrate their successes. If a New American living in poverty focuses only on the negative, he will never rise up. If an entrepreneur spends his whole day dwelling on the things he has not yet achieved or the things that did not go quite according to plan, he will never achieve anything of value.

  I have interviewed and worked with more successful CEOs than I can count, and let me tell you, they would all say the same thing: it's okay to fail. If you think you're going to get into the business of entrepreneurship without failing, you're kidding yourself. Everyone (everyone!) is bound to run into their fair share of missteps. Sometimes it's the missteps themselves that lead to success.

  So don't put too much pressure on yourself to achieve. Just do what you can to enjoy what you're doing. Believe in what you're doing. And celebrate when those things (or some portion of those things) lead to success. Start doing this and you will find that your progress will continue regardless of what happens with your various ideas. Progress is the key to momentum, and momentum is the key to small-business growth.

- Step away for a while

  Sometimes we can get so wrapped up in a problem or a goal that we lose sight of the big picture. There's that old saying that you "can't see the forest for the trees." This happens all the time in business—particularly to those who are easily distracted. It's easy to get so centered on the need to find a solution to a problem or a strategy for a goal that we begin to develop blinders. We get so set on the notion that a given solution or idea should work that we fail to see the dozens of additional solutions or ideas that might work better.

If you ever find yourself stuck, or you just can't seem to eliminate your distractions fully, Dr. Naren Gupta of Nexus Venture Partners suggests you take some time off. "When things get tough," he told me in our interview, "it is often valuable to take some time away. You don't see the obvious ways to get out of troubling situations as long as you remain in them. Only after we take a step back and get our heads clear can we examine a troubling situation completely."

As Dr. Gupta pointed out, taking some time away has a tendency to allow a business leader to clear his head. It might seem contrary to the point about momentum I made in tip three, but don't confuse a need to work all the time with actual momentum. Sometimes progress on a goal is best served when we take a step back. Taking some time away—whether for ten minutes or ten days—is often the best remedy for a particularly difficult distraction. The distraction tends to fade during the time away, and then we are free to return to the tasks at hand with new eyes and a new sense of focus.

The takeaway lesson I learned from my interviews with New American Millionaires is that focus is a constant necessity. The moment you start getting distracted—or worse, complacent—is the moment your business starts to teeter out of control. Keeping a company afloat is one of the most difficult things in the world to do. To make your entrepreneurial dreams into realities, you must be willing to dedicate thorough attention to detail at all levels and at all times.

In this chapter you learned the importance of occasionally reminding yourself of your goals. When things seem most difficult, it is always a good idea to step back, reassess what really matters to you, and then develop a plan that recenters you on only those things that matter. Do this and you will eliminate every distraction and put yourself in a better position to celebrate every success and learn from every defeat. Once you have made the lessons of this chapter a part of your life, you will be ready to absorb the next key trait in the New American Millionaire model. Read on to discover the importance of competitive drive—and, more importantly, how to make your own competitive drive work positively for you and your business.

Chapter 11

Competitive: Best Others, Better Yourself

A competitor will find a way to win. Competitors take bad breaks and use them to drive themselves just that much harder. Quitters take bad breaks and use them as reasons to give up. It's all a matter of pride.
—Nancy Lopez

The principle is competing against yourself. It's about self-improvement, about being better than you were the day before.
—Steve Young

YOU'LL NOTICE I POSTED two quotes at the head of this chapter, and they each demonstrate a different message about what it means to be competitive. There is good reason for this. When discussing successful entrepreneurs and New Americans, competitiveness often means two very different but related things.

Nancy Lopez provides the traditional definition of competitiveness: that component of striving to beat the competition no matter the cost. Inherent pride causes the competitor to do everything he can to win. Meanwhile, as Steve Young points out, a substantial component of competitiveness is a matter of self-improvement. Truly competitive people often compete within themselves to get better at everything they do. They never rest on their laurels. They are never satisfied with their accomplishments. They always strive to achieve the next thing, to meet the next goal, to improve upon what they have done in the past.

We see these two definitions of competitiveness on full display when we observe the biographies of the New American Millionaire. Successful entrepreneurs wouldn't be where they are if they hadn't done everything in their power to position their companies to be better than the rest—to win over the competition and gain as much market share as possible. They also wouldn't be who they are if they didn't find themselves constantly competing within themselves, striving to become better leaders, better innovators, better marketers, better salespeople, and better employers.

In many ways competitiveness is the key component to entrepreneurial success. Innovation, for instance, is a wonderful thing to possess, but it doesn't get you anywhere if you can't compete with yourself and with others to make that innovation a reality. For every Sergei Brin, there have been thousands of others with brilliant ideas who just were not driven enough to succeed on the same level. When posing the question about competitiveness to the New American Millionaires, I found that while they all admitted to possessing the quality—and while they all readily acknowledged it is an important value for entrepreneurs to possess—they all had different opinions of what it means to be competitive.

For Saeed Amidi of Plug and Play Tech Center, competitiveness is summed up as a need to succeed. In his opinion it's important for this competitiveness to be a key motivator in the entrepreneur's life. Whether it's financial or personal pressure—or even a pickup game of soccer—the successful entrepreneur must love to excel and need to win. It also means setting competition for yourself through goals and milestones.

"When I started Plug and Play six years ago," Amidi said, "I set in the business model the goal of having over one hundred startups in-house within the first year and a half. This was the number I believed would make us cash-flow positive, so I set that as my objective and then drove myself to achieve it. For me—and this is a lesson I learned from my father—being cash-flow positive is the ultimate goal. When you reach this point, that is when you know you have won."

For Arjun Malhotra of TechSpan and Headstrong, the competitive spirit is so ingrained he has realized he must find new ways to channel it into positive outcomes. In his early days, he would fight to win at everything—even games of Pac-Man in the office after work. Whenever competition presented itself, he would do everything in his power and practice as long as necessary to be better than everyone else.

"That's why I don't play golf," he confessed. "It would consume me."

But like any good entrepreneur, Malhotra has discovered ways to put that hyper-competitiveness to good use. He uses it in a way now that he describes as "collaborative." Where before he was driven to be the best at everything, now he is driven to train the people around him to harness their own competitive spirits.

"You have to be collaborative with your competitive nature," he explained. "You won't be around forever. So you have to leave people behind who can maintain that fire you once had."

Naren Gupta of Nexus Venture Partners has yet a third perspective on the matter. In his mind being competitive is almost entirely about being goal-oriented.

"The most difficult competition I face is the competition I have with myself," he revealed. "I don't need to satisfy anybody, but I do need to satisfy myself."

For Gupta the competition is never really over. Even when he achieves something he's been burning to reach for years, he looks at it as an opportunity and then asks himself whether he's making the best of it. "Am I leveraging everything I can?" he asks himself. "Is there anyone out there doing this better than I am? I have achieved my goals, yes, but what can I do to achieve my next goal?" For the true competitor, the question is not about accomplishments, but about what you have yet to accomplish.

In my career I have seen how a competitive spirit can run the gamut, how it can be the keenest of motivators and the most valuable of assets. Particularly in the realm of sales, a healthy dose of competitiveness is an incredibly important component of success. And yet, although I have always been extraordinarily driven and have deemed myself a go-getting, competitive individual throughout my sales career, I've found my success has always greatest when I've concentrated on competing with myself rather than with my colleagues.

I've always believed if I was able to raise the bar on myself at the completion of each of my goals, then I could ignore my concerns about whether I would best my fellow salespeople. As long as I was getting better every day at what I did, winning over the others would take care of itself. At the same time, I knew if I took my destiny in my own hands and refused to depend on others for the fulfillment of my goals, I would find myself far ahead of the competition. As an anonymous author once said, "Competing with others is arrogance. Competing with yourself is confidence!"

During much of my sales career, I formed the habit of consistently examining and scrutinizing my ongoing business model and sales figures. In this way I could build and maintain a vivid picture of my achievements—not so I could celebrate my successes, but rather so I could set greater and higher goals the moment I achieved something new. For example, I would set a financial goal for each quarter of the year. At set intervals during the quarter, I would check my progress and adjust accordingly depending on whether I was lacking, meeting, or surpassing my goals. This is what I called "competing with myself." It was my way of consistently monitoring the race I was conducting against my own expectations and my way to ensure that in the end, I always won.

New American Millionaires finds themselves keenly positioned for the competitive spirit about which I write. First, as I have already discussed, they have a tendency to dream loftier dreams than most. With this dreamer nature, they are able to see opportunities other Americans might miss. Couple that with a strong determination to succeed in this country—to never have to return home and tell their families they have failed—and it leads to a competitive spirit. For the New American, competition is a matter of pride that drives them to win at all costs—whether within themselves or against others.

While it is true that some people are more competitive than others—and true that some people are either so competitive or so noncompetitive they're detriments to themselves and their goals—it is also true that we are all competitive on some level. For those who need to cultivate a greater sense of competition and those who might need to rein it in a little, the steps are essentially the same. Read on for further thoughts on the value of competitiveness and how to make it work in your favor.

- Keep it positive

  There are two sides to competitiveness. On one hand, a competitive person can compete in such a way as to improve himself positively. On the other hand, a competitive person might strive simply to take away from others in order to gain some kind of advantage.

  The goal here should be to work more toward the former. When we strive to take knowledge from others or control the way others work or play, we are using our competitive nature in a negative fashion. The trouble with thinking this way is that it tends to close your mind to new possibilities. It hones you down to the point where you are focusing entirely on beating those who are better than you at something, no matter what, and shuts you out from the potential to learn from those people.

  If you hope to build a better business or create a better product, you must channel your competition into something that advances you in a positive way. Compete not to beat your coworkers or mentors; compete to gain as much knowledge from them as possible. Don't work to get better numbers than everyone else; work to absorb their knowledge and advantages into your own game plan. Ask questions. Acquire new strategies. Learn and strive to be better.

- Never stop achieving

As Amidi pointed out, competition is only truly valuable if it is ongoing. A business cannot grow and thrive if its leader ever gets complacent. He must always strive for the next victory or for that next opportunity to get better at what he and his company do. Do not be satisfied with the end of an outcome or the achievement of a goal; be satisfied only in the journey. Relish not the winning but the competition itself. Do this and you will find yourself trying harder, achieving more, and realizing greater success than you ever thought possible.

- Stay humble

The hyper-competitive often have what armchair psychiatrists might describe as huge egos. These are exactly what drive them to win in the first place—that need to be better than everyone else, that need to reinforce one's self-image through repeated and overwhelming victory. The problem with this kind of competition is that it tends to drive people away. It makes a person more difficult to work with and can even tarnish the reputation of an otherwise valuable company.

Remaining competitive is incredibly important for successful entrepreneurship, but competitiveness without humility is rarely a positive thing. If you interview as many entrepreneurs as I have, you will find a rather universal observation emerging: for as successful as these people are—for as many millions as they have amassed and for as many lives as they have touched— they are almost always humble about it. They don't trumpet their successes. Often it's a chore just to get them to talk about the things they have achieved.

For them it's never a matter of what they have done personally. They always point out how much help they had and often tend to dwell on how much work is yet to be done. It's an interesting component, and one that can be emulated easily. Sure, winning is important, and learning is important, but if you're incapable of winning and learning graciously, then you will soon find yourself working alone.

- Create and seek out competition wherever you can
This final tip speaks again to the idea that successful people are never complacent. We know most New American Millionaires tend to concentrate all their efforts on the next goal rather than celebrating the goals they have already achieved. But what happens when it appears they have reached the top? What happens when you're Amazon.com and you find you are the biggest bookseller in the world? What happens when you gain the entire market for your business in your hometown?

The answer to the first question is that you branch out. If you're Amazon, you don't settle for being the biggest bookseller in the world; you strive to become *the* online marketplace—the site where everyone goes to shop for literally anything they can think of. The answer to the second question is that you seek out new competition. You don't settle for being the top fish in your current pond; you go someplace where the competition is better. You recognize competition is what betters you personally, and so you never stop working to find newer and better people with whom to compete—and from whom you can learn. This is exactly the reason you find such huge collections of similarly skilled people in the same geographical locations. If you want great jazz, you go to New Orleans. If you want great fashion, you go to New York. If you want to make or star in a movie, you go to Los Angeles. If you want to become the next tech giant, you set up your business in Silicon Valley.

Competitive people are always drawn to the inspiration and potential for personal growth that comes from surrounding themselves with other competitive and skilled people. The concept is as true in business as it is in sports. If you want to get better at golf, you don't play someone with a thirty handicap;

you play the club pro. So, if you find yourself having trouble finding new competition, change the venue. Surround yourself with people with greater skill and more knowledge than yourself. This is the only way to better yourself and to use your competitiveness in a productive way.

Competitiveness can be an entrepreneur's greatest asset or his most significant hindrance. It's all a matter of how he chooses to use it. With the steps above—and with careful consideration of how your competitiveness is viewed by others—you will be well on your way to turning your competitive spirit in a positive direction. You will constantly strive to be better at what you do, and the resultant success will come naturally.

In this chapter you learned how to keep your competitive spirit positive. Most importantly you learned that the best entrepreneurs are never fully satisfied with what they have at present. Even when an achievement is reached, the competition does not end. A great business leader always strives for that next piece of success, always looks for that next opportunity to better himself.

With that in mind, a successful entrepreneur is also capable of recognizing that sometimes other people are in better positions to achieve. The New American Millionaire is extremely competitive, but he is also capable of allowing the people around him to compete on his company's behalf. In the next chapter, you will learn the secrets of how some of the world's most successful entrepreneurs make the most of their productive capacity by delegating to the people they trust.

Chapter 12

Delegator: How to Get 48 Hours' Work Out of Every Day

*If you perform a task that someone else can do, you
keep yourself from a task that only you can do.*
—Barbara Volpe and Paula Jorde Bloom

*The best executive is the one who has sense enough to pick
good men to do what he wants done and self-restraint enough
to keep from meddling with them while they do it.*
—Theodore Roosevelt

EVEN BEFORE I SET foot on this continent, the thing I admired most about Americans was their self-reliant spirit. It is, in a sense, what built this country. The first immigrants to these shores came because they believed it was the only place where their ideas would be allowed to take root and flourish. The pioneers moved west in an attempt to carve out their livelihoods in a land untouched by civilization and the strictures therein. These brave and intrepid souls would make new lives

125

for themselves—building new homes, establishing new businesses, raising whole cities from the ground up—and they would do it all on their own. There would be no help from others. If you wanted something done, you had to do it yourself.

This pathos was further cemented during the Industrial Revolution, when the titans of industry were so widely celebrated for their can-do spirit. Every news source seemed to treat the Andrew Carnegies and John D. Rockefellers of the world like champions—men who built the industrial machines of this country with their own bare hands. Even today their leadership is celebrated in all the history books.

But the truth is, if you look back and study the rise of industry in America (and all the other major economic and political advancements either before or since), it seems pretty clear the idea that one man can raise a mega-corporation on his own is a little ridiculous. To think Carnegie and Rockefeller juggled all the tasks it takes to build an empire is a fallacy. Of course they had help. And so has every other major entrepreneur who created a multimillion (or multibillion) dollar company.

This is where the New American Millionaire might hold another advantage over the average American entrepreneur. Where the American was born in a country that has always celebrated self-reliance, the New American Millionaire is that much better equipped (and willing) to ask for help. What I mean when I write "ask for help"—at least in the business sense—is that a good entrepreneur knows which tasks to keep for himself and which to delegate to others. He recognizes that business ventures are incredibly complicated things. And while he may well believe no one can manage his tasks better than he can, he is also equipped with the understanding that sometimes the greater good is better served if he allows someone else to manage various tasks in his stead. He works hard, yes. But he also encourages those who work for and with him to work hard as well—oftentimes on his behalf.

If you interview as many CEOs as I have, it becomes immediately clear that no successful businessperson gets by on his work alone. If one were to sit down and attempt to complete all the many tasks for which a

CEO is responsible in a given day, one would need more than a twenty-four-hour day with which to work. The expectations heaped upon the man or woman in charge are such that even twice that many hours would not suffice. In other words, CEOs *need* people they can trust to assume some of their tasks for them. They need to delegate. And what separates the successful CEOs from the less successful is how *effectively* they do so. It's not how much work they're willing or able to manage on their own that matters. It's how much they're willing and able to assign to others (and how well they coach, motivate, and follow up with these others) that matters.

I learned this lesson the hard way. As I became more advanced in the financial services industry, I began to handle more substantial monies for high net-worth individuals and companies. I went from being a junior advisor to working as a portfolio manager. This entailed preparing investment analyses for clients, including several with more than $50 million in total assets under management.

Other assignments included communicating with sell-side analysts and company management, assessing economic trends, and selecting and monitoring investments in various securities and money instruments. In a sense it was like I had absorbed the work of four people, where before I'd had to worry about the work of only one. I had always worked hard, of course. But now, with so many responsibilities, I would have to learn to work smart as well.

The first step toward working smart is accepting that everyone has limitations—yourself included. For me I found two areas in which I felt less adept in terms of performance. The more I thought about them, the more it became clear that I would save a great deal of time and increase my own efficiency if I allowed myself to rely upon the services of others in the company who had proven themselves proficient. My two areas most in need of delegation included conducting company research and analyzing profiles. Fortunately there were many junior advisors at my firm who were quite capable and seasoned in accomplishing these tasks. What I needed to do was figure out a way to bring these advisors into the fold with me, motivate them to help, and establish a system wherein productive work and clear follow-up could occur.

Through some trial and error, I did manage to develop a system of delegation that worked well for me. Not only did my own productivity increase, but the numbers for my new team did as well. Together we were able to manage more money and make better investment decisions than I ever could have on my own. My new team of advisors also helped to identify a number of startups that yielded significant returns for our clientele. The decision to delegate turned out to be a win for everyone involved.

That's the wonderful thing about delegation. It makes *everyone* more efficient. As the quote at the head of this chapter suggests, it frees you up to do the things only you can do. And as an added bonus, it relieves stress in the process.

The successful entrepreneur knows how to assign tasks to people who can handle them—and in so doing frees up more of his day to focus on the more intricate or delicate elements of business management. Truly successful entrepreneurs are so good at delegation that the work they provide boasts the quality and quantity of what you might normally expect from a team of ten people. And yet sometimes, when you look at these same successful entrepreneurs, it seems like they're not really working at all. They've just gotten so good at delegation they seem to pass without effort through the staggering amount of work for which they are responsible.

New American Philsophy: Why Doesn't Everyone Do It?

It seems so easy, doesn't it? This key element to success in entrepreneurship requires only that you make yourself willing to assign some of your work to others. The act of delegating promises to make you more effective and your business more efficient. Who wouldn't want that? A fairly substantial number of aspiring business leaders, it would seem...

For many people—and this is particularly true of the kinds of people who dream of becoming millionaires—it is quite difficult to give up even one ounce of control. Aspiring millionaires are simply more apt to believe no one can do what they do better than they can. For this reason they have a tendency to want (and sometimes need) to manage everything on their own. Relinquishing control to others can be a terrifying prospect.

It's difficult to blame them. Many times the person in charge has far more experience with leadership tasks than those with whom he works. And experience almost always leads to a higher quality of work. Plus, if you think about it, it seems perfectly logical to assume a given task can be done more quickly if the person in charge manages it himself. Why would he want to take all that time to contact someone he trusts, bring them up to speed on the issue, explain to them what he expects of them, and then wait for them to finish performing the work? Given all he knows and has experienced, it would seem if the person in charge kept the task himself, it would lead to a higher-quality result in less time.

And on top of that, if he decides to delegate to someone else, what happens if that person fails to perform the task correctly? Then the delegator would be left with an unresolved issue, would have lost a great deal of time, and (worse yet) would have a whole host of additional mistakes to address. In a sense this scenario would lead to the given task taking far longer. It would require more effort for the delegator to right the wrongs than it might have if he had just managed the task from the beginning on his own.

The above concerns are only natural. I've experienced many of them myself. So have a great many of the successful entrepreneurs I have interviewed. All these concerns are based on a person's ability to trust those who work for him or with him. But many of us have trouble with trust. We feel there is no way to assure that the person in whom we are placing our trust will live up to our expectations. We fear that if they don't, we'll wind up looking bad.

So the goal here in becoming a better delegator is to establish a system that will allow us to expand our capacity to trust. Through that system we can finally let go of our need to control and can reap the tremendous benefits that result from proper and carefully considered delegation.

No one can manage a million-dollar business on their own (at least not without going crazy). To be a successful entrepreneur, you must be willing to delegate. You must understand delegation isn't just about dropping the work you don't want to do onto others; it's about identifying which tasks are best managed on your own and which are best assigned to others. It's about managing the work others perform on your behalf. It's about ensuring that the people who work with and for you are in the best positions to get the job done efficiently and effectively. And, most of all, it's about freeing yourself up to concentrate on the more challenging or pressing tasks—the key decisions that will determine the success or failure of your business ventures and, of course, the things at which you excel.

If you can learn to become an effective delegator, your productive capacity will improve. Just as importantly, so will the productive capacity of the people to whom you delegate. Everyone in whom you place your trust will be able to expand their knowledge base, thereby improving their ability to contribute to the overall business. This will make everyone in the operation more effective, productive, knowledgeable, and efficient. It will transform your company from a place run by a single expert into a place that progresses via the combined efforts of many experts. And when this happens, the sky is the limit.

So, with all of that in mind, let's move on to the lessons of the New American Millionaire on how to delegate effectively.

- Assess your work and your workers
  There are many reasons to delegate—some of them right and some of them wrong. The wrong reasons include being too stressed or you just don't want to deal with a particular task. Taking something you don't want to do and sticking it with someone else (regardless of that person's capacity to manage the task) isn't delegation. That's just laziness. Effective delegation

requires that you thoughtfully consider which tasks might be better served by someone else. And the only way to determine which tasks can be delegated versus kept is to assess the work you have on hand carefully.

First make a list of all the work you must perform this week. Then determine which tasks are more administrative in nature. This is the busy work—the work that does not require a high level of leadership to accomplish. Because this work is often less decision-intensive, it does not require your leadership skills. If you were to keep it for yourself, it would merely bog you down. It's also more likely that it can be performed satisfactorily by someone you trust. Consider all the administrative work on your docket as work that can be delegated.

Next determine which of the remaining tasks will require the most of your time. Some of these tasks may require high-level decisions to be made. Some may not. The frequency and amount of those high-level decisions is what you will use to determine whether the task can be delegated or not. Remember, your decision-making skills are valuable, but so is your time. Often, delegating the more time-intensive tasks frees you up for things that are even more important.

Assess the people with whom you work. Tasks that can be delegated might not make themselves apparent until you carefully consider the skill sets of the people on whom you rely. That new employee might benefit from some of the administrative work, for example. Someone in sales who might become a better worker by crossing over into tasks often associated with marketing. Your assigning a particular person to take your place as liaison to a given client or partner company might expand their capabilities as a leader.

As a final note on the assessment step, serial entrepreneur Rajan Raghavan made a particularly important point in our interview: delegating is a whole lot easier if you surround yourself with people who are not only smart but smarter than you.

"Very soon you realize you cannot do everything yourself," he says. "I've found that relying on people who are smarter than you is the best practice because they can often do things in ways that you are not capable of."

The bottom line when assessing candidates for delegation is that you should never delegate a task to a person if he cannot be expected to manage it. If his skill set is such that he will need to stretch to meet expectations, then don't assign him the work. If you expect he's too busy to meet a deadline, then don't assign him the work. Effective delegation isn't simply about spreading the work around; it's about assessing which work would fit which people in the most effective ways. Assign out as much of your work as possible, but don't set up the assignees to fail.

At **www.milliondollarsuccessinstitute.com**, I offer a questionnaire designed to assess which of your employees or coworkers are best suited for any given task as well as a strategy that will help you manage your various delegated assignments.

- Be clear
  More often than not, the difference between success and failure of a delegated task is a matter of communication. If you don't communicate clearly to your assignee on all that you expect of him, how can you expect him to perform to your satisfaction? Not even the most capable workers are mind readers.

  Do not be afraid to spend as much time as you need to go over everything in detail. Don't skimp on the descriptions of what you expect to be achieved. Point out the potential problems or pitfalls the assignee might expect to encounter. Tell him in detail about the outcomes you hope to achieve by the end of the task. Perhaps most importantly, be sure to explain not just the *what* but the *why* of the task you are delegating. Many times the assignee will give a greater effort if he understands why the given work is necessary. If he understands the rewards as well as the outcomes, he will work that much harder to achieve them.

Clarity cannot be properly achieved through simple dictation, however. As with almost every business decision (or life decision, for that matter), questions are absolutely critical. When assigning a task to someone else, be sure to give him ample time to ask questions of you. There is simply no better way to ensure your message is fully received. And when you're finished fielding questions, be sure to ask a few of your own. Once your message has been fully delivered, ask the assignee to reiterate how he plans to attack the task at hand.

Sometimes it's best to think of delegation more as an open and honest conversation.

"I don't really delegate tasks," Gabriel Nossovitch of WorldWorks Inc. said. "When I have work to assign out, we have an open and frank discussion on what needs to happen. We divide the initiatives and decide who will tackle what on a week-to-week basis. The process is based on a deep understanding of what value each person brings to the table."

He is also quick to point out that clarity sometimes comes at a price. "Sometimes you will have disagreements. Sometimes you will have to insist that the other person does the work you would like them to do."

But proper delegation—delegation that is open, honest, and delivered in a noncondescending way—almost always leads to effective work management. "These disagreements are rare if the focus is always on deciding how you can best serve the people to whom you delegate. It's a matter of determining who has the best skill to meet a given task," said Nossovitch.

Special note: Another great tip is to get correspondence in writing. While it is always more effective to delegate a task face to face, full clarity is often achieved only after the communication is made in writing as well. People tend to interpret the spoken word differently from the written word. Providing the assignee with both spoken and written representations of the task at hand is a great way to ensure he achieves full understanding. Once he has gotten more experienced in the work, future iterations of the task can be assigned simply via e-mail. Allowing for questions and follow-up remains important, but delivering the matter face to face becomes less so.

- Accept the possibility of setbacks
Sure, you're a capable individual. Your efforts have led to the realization of success in business. But you obviously didn't get to where you are without making at least a few mistakes. You have had shortfalls. You have had setbacks. You have had failures. So expecting anything else from your assignees would be folly.

    If you assign some of your work to other people, you will of course encounter a few setbacks. The work you assign might come back wrong. There might be mistakes you have to fix. It could be that your assignee misunderstood what you wanted entirely. It could be that this misunderstanding will lead to a major issue in the project.

    Try to remain positive. If you expect these things to occur, they will be less devastating when they inevitably do. And if you remain positive, you avoid the added risk of alienating the assignee. Instead of assaulting him with accusations or unreasonable demands, understand that this—as is the case with everything in life—is a learning process. Point out where he fell short of your expectations. Explain exactly how he can do things differently next time. Be assertive but gentle. And do everything you can to maintain your assignee's confidence.

- Stick with it
Once you have delegated a task to another person, the worst thing you can do is assume it's completely out of your hands. Many times your assignee will have questions. Sometimes these are questions only you can answer. Some leaders might simply say, "It's your responsibility now. Figure it out yourself." But there is no surer way to disaster on a delegated task. While requiring self-reliance might lead an assignee to expand his

capabilities and knowledge base quicker, it also could lead to resentment or a shortfall in performance.

"You cannot delegate responsibly until you have systems in place," said entrepreneur Rajan Raghavan. "You have to have a regular cadence of meetings and a regular cadence of reports. You have to delve into many of the details, but at the same time you have to be comfortable enough for other people to make decisions. You need to empower the people under you to be able to succeed."

So, when you delegate, remain committed to the task from start to finish. Remember, it's still ultimately your responsibility. Encourage your assignees to provide regular progress reports. Ask questions throughout the process (and answer them too). Set clear goals and outcomes and remind your assignees when a given goal or outcome is coming due. And when the task is complete, provide a thorough, comprehensive review.

Special note: If you've reached the end of the first cycle of a task performed by an assignee, it is often best practice to perform your final review in his presence. Assuming you remain positive and informative throughout the review, the assignee will learn more about expectations and opportunities to improve if he is allowed to witness the review in person. He will see more directly your thought process on the task, will learn a great deal more about the reasons *why* you expect a certain level or manner of performance, and will be able to ask and answer illuminating questions about the task.

You have expected your assignee to be hands-on and as self-reliant as possible on this task from the start, so there is no reason not to include him in the finish. He has helped you to complete the task. You would do well to allow him to help you to assess the outcome.

- Reward successes and fix shortfalls
  As you assess the outcome of the task, be sure to point out areas where the assignee excelled. Praise him for these successes. Where

possible, reward him as well. In areas where improvement is needed, be sure to provide constructive feedback. The key word here is *constructive*. It's okay to point out flaws in the approach, but do so in the most positive fashion possible. Where there have been shortfalls, it's better to discuss what went wrong than to point the finger. Ask the assignee to explain what he believes he needs to perform better. Use what he tells you to construct a better plan of attack for the next time around.

In the end, if you can learn to delegate effectively, your company will become much more efficient and extraordinarily more capable. Trust the people around you and you will take your company to new heights.

Remember, though, you should not expect your assignees to perform in exactly the same way you do. There are many ways to achieve a positive outcome. Some may differ from yours. If you can accept that fact—if you can properly assess which people are best suited for which tasks, if you can communicate the needs of the task clearly and effectively, and if you can be patient and positive with your assignees—then you will be well on your way to delegating like a New American Millionaire.

When you have absorbed the lessons of this chapter and made them a part of your life, you will be ready to move on to the final piece of the entrepreneurial puzzle. You have learned ten of the eleven key traits of the New American Millionaire. Read on to discover how finding ultimate success is often a matter of realizing the lessons presented by each day on the job.

Chapter 13

Education: Learn to Learn in Your Everyday Life

*Education is what remains after one has
forgotten everything he learned in school.*
—Albert Einstein

*Formal education will make you a living;
self-education will make you a fortune.*
—Jim Rohn

*Any man is educated who knows where to get knowledge when he needs it
and how to organize that knowledge into definite plans of action.*
—Napoleon Hill

IT SEEMS ONLY FITTING that our chapters on the most common characteristics shared by New Americans and millionaire entrepreneurs should end with the matter of education. I say it's fitting because, of all the characteristics I have shared in this book, this is the one with the broadest and most encompassing meaning.

You might notice the three quotes I have listed at the head of this chapter refer to education not in its traditional terms but rather in its everyday application. This is the true beauty of the education an entrepreneur requires: while a college degree certainly helps, it pales in comparison to the vast and valuable knowledge the observant, the innovative, the adventurous, and the focused can glean from their personal experiences. It is a beautiful thing—truly a uniquely American possibility.

Of all the traits that make the New American Millionaire, this is perhaps the most often overlooked. Matters of education are so often assumed. If a man or woman is successful and rich, we just tend to assume that he or she most likely went to college. But the education I mean to outline in this book is not the one you gain in the classroom. It is the one you gain in your chosen field. More often than not, what separates the successful from the also-rans is a keen ability to learn from mistakes, successes, the people around them, and competing businesses. As Vinod Khosla explained, "Where most entrepreneurs fail is on the things they don't know they don't know." Those who survive are the ones who never stop striving to learn all those things they don't know.

Nearly every millionaire entrepreneur I interviewed for this book came to America for roughly the same reason: the higher education in this country is widely considered to be second to none. Masood Kermani chose to continue his studies in this country because his father revered the education he might receive here. Henry Wong made the leap from Hong Kong because his options in his home country were just so much more limited than they are in the US. Naren Gupta arrived on these shores because he believed that nowhere else in the world could he get such a respected advanced degree. But this should come as no surprise. The American secondary education system is admired the world over.

What might come as a surprise is that none of these business leaders would rate their formal education as more important than the valuable knowledge they gained *outside* the walls of their classrooms. It seems that a common belief held among New American Millionaires is that the best entrepreneurial education comes from trial and error, from learning from one's peers, and from hitting the ground running with a new and risky company.

This is good news. What it means is that one does not necessarily need a college education to reach the top of one's industry. While that college education certainly provides a head start, it is entirely possible to gain all the wisdom and knowledge one needs to be a successful entrepreneur simply by learning from one's experiences and listening to the people one meets and works alongside. In college you don't necessarily learn what it takes to build a business, delegate effectively to a capable staff, or make an innovation soar from idea to wildly successful product. You don't learn the logistics of how to expand your supply lines or partner with a company that shares your strategic goals. You learn these things in the trenches—or, more often than not, in the coffee shop. You learn these things by experiencing them directly, not by reading about them in textbooks.

It is interesting to note that a substantial percentage of the entrepreneurs I interviewed did not cite their college choices as the most important elements of their educational success. Instead they pointed to the regions of the country in which they ended up doing business. For most of those I interviewed, that region is Silicon Valley. Entrepreneur after entrepreneur sang the praises of America's greatest hotbed of technology innovation. Even when asked what they appreciated most about their opportunities in the US, many revealed an appreciation not just for the country as a whole but for Silicon Valley in particular.

"Silicon Valley is the best place in the world to start a company," Wong revealed. "The region is more than just a patch of real estate. It's an essence. It's a place where people build things together. Here you can draw out an idea on a napkin while you sit with a colleague in a restaurant. You can create the vision for a new company over lunch. You can lay the groundwork of a new and innovative idea literally anywhere and at any time simply because you happen to be surrounded by all the people you need to make that idea a reality."

"I feel very fortunate to have had the opportunity to live here and be a part of this community," Saeed Amidi shared. "Still, even today, with all the struggle we have seen in this country, America and Silicon Valley provide the best platform for someone to expand their personal education and build their career, life, and success."

This concept points to the simple fact that, when it comes to education, environment is the most important factor. It isn't the school at which you study; it is the people with whom you surround yourself. Successful CEOs like Amidi and Wong believe they owe much of their success to the environment in which they do business.

I have to admit these kinds of thoughts hadn't occurred to me before I began the interview process in support of this book. Even though I have lived in Silicon Valley for years, it had not occurred to me how important the environment itself was to my success. It is from our environment that we all gain the most valuable components of our education. The more innovative the environment, the more innovative we will become. The more successful the people we surround ourselves with, the more successful we will become. The concept is so natural that, at first, I overlooked it. It is so natural that I failed to recognize how my own life had been proof of this fact from the time I first left university.

Being an international student, when I'd started school I was classified as a nonresident for the purpose of university fee apportionment. It did not take me long to realize this would make the cost of my education prohibitive. When I'd dropped out of school, I'd done so out of necessity, and because I'd still held on to the belief that a formal education is the most important thing a man can possess, I'd told myself the dropping out would be only a temporary matter. One day soon, when I could afford it, I would return to complete my education.

Of course there were complications to this plan. The act of dropping out proved to be a threat to my continued legal immigration status in the US. The law required foreign students to be enrolled full-time in school. If absent for more than two consecutive semesters, I would face deportation procedures. I knew if I could not return to my university in that allotted timeframe, the authorities at the school would report my noncompliance to the INS.

Nevertheless, there seemed to be little that I could do. Money was tight and I simply could not make my tuition payments without a steadier and higher-paying job. So, in the end, risking deportation was a chance I was willing to take. The hardships I had endured had pushed me to my limits. I knew now that I had to do whatever it would take to dig out of the hole I had created for myself. As far as the consequences were concerned, I would cross that bridge when I came to it.

Before I reached this final analysis, I was able to meet with my mentor, who explained to me that there is more than one way to find monetary success in America. He believed he could show me a different kind of education that would allow me to succeed in the field of business even without an advanced degree. I absorbed everything my mentor had to teach me. I used his business processes and strategies as a model, adopting them into my sales approach. And, to my great surprise, in almost no time at all I experienced the same level of success that had changed my mentor's life. I found that my success in this new sales career depended not just on what I could learn in the classroom but on the mastery of a large body of new knowledge I would gain through successful (and unsuccessful) sales pitches, meetings, and ventures with my fellow sales staff.

What I discovered in those years was that formal education is not the absolute key to success. Rather it's the most important precursor to a disciplined life. Formal education is not necessarily a means to an end. Instead, it is as Napoleon Hill pointed out in the third quote at the head of this chapter. Formal education doesn't teach you all the skills and knowledge you will need to succeed in life; it teaches you *how to find* those skills and that knowledge.

With all of that in mind—and since I cannot possibly hope to offer you an advanced degree through the pages of this book—let's examine the kinds of things to look for in your pursuit of that special brand of life and work education that has propelled so many New Americans to success.

- Find a mentor
  While it is true that it's possible to learn many of the most important things in life on our own, it is also true that it's far more likely for us to learn them (and learn them well) if they are

taught to us by someone who was there before us. You could not have expected to learn to speak, read and write, or ride a bicycle without the influence and guidance of your parents. In much the same way, you cannot expect to learn the secrets of success in your chosen field without the advice of a person who knows those secrets already and has lived them every day.

When it comes to advancing one's knowledge in a given field, there is nothing like a mentor. You could try your ideas and your strategies from scratch if you like, but it's often the case that the sum of a mentor's experience can save you from a great deal of error and setback. If you can find someone who has been in your shoes before and who has demonstrated success over many years, you will have access to a wealth of incredibly valuable (and, more importantly, relevant) ideas that will help you build your business and realize similar success.

This is all well and good in theory, but the practice of finding a mentor is another thing entirely. Not everyone is fortunate enough to cross paths with someone who is willing and able to lend them their ear—not to mention the knowledge that might well give them their competitive advantage in the first place. Mentors like the one who helped me realize success are a rare and valuable breed. For this reason it helps to know where to look, and how to initiate the relationship.

Where to look is simple: the best mentors are leaders in their fields. Notice I say "leaders" and not "*the* leaders." Often the top leaders in a field will be so busy with work that they will not have the time it takes to mentor someone they have only just met. Additionally I suspect the Sergei Brins of the world receive several hundred (if not thousand) requests for mentorship every week. There are, however, plenty of top minds in every field, and many would be willing to help you. It's just a matter of knowing how to ask.

Oftentimes the best approach is simply to pick up the phone and ask. Other times the potential mentor might prefer to build up a working relationship before he or she will be willing to share the most valuable portions of his or her knowledge. In these cases consider approaching the situation not as a newcomer to the field seeking a mentor but as an entrepreneur with an idea that will require a strategic partnership. Let the prospective mentor know how much you value his or her insight and expertise. Explain that your concept would not be possible without his or her input and aid. Whenever possible offer the prospective mentor a valued service in return. In other words do something for him or her before you ever ask him or her to do something for you.

Finding a candidate for mentor is easy, but making that candidate an actual mentor is a little like making a new friend. These things take time. They can't be rushed into. Relationships like these are built on a series of shared experiences. Increase your opportunity to share experiences with your prospective mentor and in no time you will find yourself in line to receive his or her valuable knowledge and insight.

- Absorb all the lessons your mentor (or even your idols) has to offer
In the case of your mentor, never be afraid to ask questions—even when they seem ridiculous. Pick his or her brain about *everything* that seems relevant. Ask for advice. Ask for help. Ask your mentor to explain to you how he or she might handle the situation that stands before you. Ask him or her about the mistakes he or she has made. In this way you can avoid making the same mistakes.

You might have noticed I included the word *idols* in this tip. What I mean by that is all those people in your field (or similar fields) who have realized the kind of success you hope to find one day. If your goal is politics, study the wisdom of the presidents you most admire. If your goal is to succeed in the technology sector, read every article you can about the champions of that industry. Sometimes the best advice can be found in the headlines and doesn't have to come from face-to-face interaction. Study those people you admire most, and never be afraid to emulate.

- Read as much as you can
  If ever you need a piece of specialized knowledge that your mentor can't provide (or that you can't glean on your own in the absence of a mentor), there's nothing like a book to bridge the gap. And the beautiful thing about books is you don't need to be enrolled in a college to access them. In fact you don't even need money. In today's hyper-competitive and hyper-fast business world, the library is still one of the most valuable places an entrepreneur can frequent. If you need tips on marketing, you can find everything you need to know in a library. If you need the records of market trends and financials in your industry, you can find them at the library. If you're just looking to broaden your horizons on a field you hope to enter into, there's always the library.

  If you polled one hundred CEOs about their study habits, you would be blown away by the sheer number of books they read. Some suggest they read as much as a full book *each day*. This means that every day they're learning something new and profound about the world and the industry in which they work. Imagine the kind of advantage that brings. So why in the world would you deprive yourself of this same advantage? Books expand your knowledge and your abilities. They make you a better person and a brighter business leader. And they can be had absolutely free. Read often. Read always. Read as much as you can.

- Don't just learn—do
  Many entrepreneurs find themselves failing simply because they spend too much time trying to study and learn about their industry and concepts. When it comes to life lessons, there is simply no substitute for good, old-fashioned trial and error. Mentors can teach you about their successes and mistakes.

Idols can demonstrate a clear path to success. Books can show you best practices. But none of these things can teach you the valuable lesson of *how* to make an idea work in your unique field, environment, marketplace, and circumstance. Many entrepreneurs have come before you. Many great ideas have been launched from concept to corporation. But none of these entrepreneurs were you. And none of these great ideas were yours. This makes you unique, and because you are unique your path to success will be unique as well. You will share similarities with others, certainly, but it is the differences you must learn about.

So find a mentor. Emulate a hero. Read as much as you can. And when you have done all this, put your knowledge into action. Once the wheels are turning on your idea or strategy, the true learning can begin.

The most important thing about an entrepreneur's education isn't just that it's all around; it's that it never ends. Even after you have begun to realize success with your new product or company, understand that you must continue to learn. The entrepreneur who gets complacent, who gets satisfied with his or her current standing in the world, is destined for a hard fall from the top. The learning process is perpetual and ongoing. Even when your education has become broad enough to get you to the top, you have to work on expanding that education in order to remain there. The world and the marketplace are always changing. If you never stop learning, you can ensure that you always change right along with it.

Chapter 14

Thinking Ahead

Action will remove the doubt that theory cannot solve.
—Pehyl Hsieh

YOU HAVE REACHED THE end of this book, and if you're feeling at all like I was feeling when I first experienced the epiphany that led to the New American Millionaire process, you are probably asking yourself one question: what do I do now? This is a question all entrepreneurs ask themselves at one time or another, and it is a question with a singular answer: you must *act*. You must take all of the lessons you have learned in these pages and all the wisdom imparted by the New American Millionaires who contributed to this book, and you must shape them into a plan that works for you and your unique business.

From the bottom of my heart, I hope you have enjoyed reading about the lessons I have learned over many years of entrepreneurial experience and research. More importantly I hope you have found something within these pages that has inspired you to do something great, to make your dream a reality and to change your way of thinking to reflect the key traits that make a millionaire entrepreneur so successful. Remember, reaching the end of this book is only the first step in the process. Now it's up to you to take the lessons you've learned and make them a part of your entrepreneurial reality.

In the first half of this book, you learned to spend and save as if you were starting out in a new country and not just a new business. You discovered how to maximize your resources in times of deficit as well as surplus. If you can think about your funding and other resources as a matter of survival and not just a matter of making ends meet, you will have a huge leg up as you move toward becoming cash-flow positive.

I revealed that the mark of a true entrepreneur is a certain fearlessness and spirit of adventure. The more you begin thinking about your business—and the various decisions you must make in support of that business—as chances and not risks, the better your decisions will become. The fearless and adventurous understand that nothing worth doing in life is without risk, and the greatest rewards are always reserved for those who are willing to take the leap.

Through the lessons of my New American Millionaire contributors, you gained insight into the benefits of being, thinking, and acting as an outsider. Often the difference between a successful business and an unsuccessful one is as simple as how brilliantly the enterprise stands out from the crowd. More than anything the first half of this book showed that, in order to think like a New American Millionaire and in order to achieve your dreams, you must possess a burning desire unrivaled in your field. You have learned the steps you will need to get your business off the ground. If you wish to keep it there, you have to want it more than the competition, and you have to keep wanting it even when you encounter the inevitable setbacks.

In the second half of this book, you gained valuable insight into the mindset that leads to innovation. Yahoo!, Sun Microsystems, and Google would not be where they are today without heavy and frequent doses of remarkable innovation. That starts at the top. That starts with you, and it is furthered by the smart and capable people with whom you choose to surround yourself.

You learned that two of the greatest keys to entrepreneurial success are remaining focused despite consistent distraction and figuring out how to harness your competitive drive with both the competition and yourself. You discovered that the thing that separates great leaders from good ones is an ability and willingness to delegate to trusted colleagues.

Finally I shared the knowledge that the most successful companies in the world are led by people who understand that an entrepreneur—even one who has reached the pinnacle of success in his or her venture—never stops learning. Everything in life and in business is a learning opportunity. Those who choose to accept and celebrate that fact find themselves in much better positions to adapt their businesses and survive.

With all these lessons at hand, you now have nearly everything you need to overcome even the harshest of economic climates. While many Americans both new and old struggle to find jobs or launch businesses in these trying times, you will find yourself in a position to succeed. There is no mistaking that you have the knowledge. You have the insight. I have held back nothing of the wisdom provided to me by some of America's most successful entrepreneurs. The only thing you are missing at this point is the action.

So what do you do next? You must commit to the steps I have outlined in each chapter. When I write *commit*, I mean true commitment. It's not enough to read them. It's not even enough to memorize them. You must absorb them into your daily routine. You must accept them and make them a part of your life. You must do the work they describe and you must do it diligently. Why? Because without commitment and without action you will not experience the change in mindset required to think like a New American Millionaire. Without commitment and without action, you are likely to return to the comfort zone to which you have become accustomed. You will miss out on all the great and dramatic change the New American Millionaire process offers.

My life is testament to how the New American Millionaire process can work for you. I began as a poor, young college student with hardly a grasp of the language, let alone an understanding of how to navigate the entrepreneurial landscape of this country. Through my trials and tribulations, I leaned on the wisdom inherent in my upbringing and as a result have reached a level of success I never could have dreamed of as a child.

I am not the only one either. All individuals interviewed for this book—and hundreds more not included in these pages—got to where they are because they displayed the eleven traits of the New American Millionaire. You have read the wisdom of some of the wealthiest and most successful entrepreneurs working in this country. All have expressed thanks for the opportunities they were able to find in the land of the free. All of them owe their success to a keen ability to innovate, motivate (themselves and others), and never give up in the face of difficulty.

You face your own difficulty at the time of this writing. We all do. The global economy has led to an entrepreneurial landscape that is anything but stable. Great companies are built overnight, and established companies are destroyed just as quickly. But even though the world has changed, the path to success has not. It may have become more difficult, yes, but the champions of the New American Millionaire process do not shy away from difficulty. They take whatever steps are necessary to further their goal of reaching the top. They take action. And they take action *now*.

In furtherance of this point, I am thrilled to offer you an opportunity to take real and measurable action in the pursuit of your dreams. The first step is to visit my website: **www.MillionDollarSuccessInstitute. com** and click on the link for your free gifts. The gifts include:

- A most valuable and downloadable MP3 recording of my interview with Mike Litman, the # 1bestselling author of *Conversations with Millionaires.*
- My eBook, *Success is in the mind.*
- A coupon for a ten percent discount for my MASTERY online training program, the *Million Dollar Success Institute*

Each of the tools above will aid you on your journey toward thinking like a New American Millionaire. Each will inspire you to absorb the knowledge you have gained in these pages and put that knowledge to work for all your business ventures. Each of them certainly helped me as I began to claw my way out of my dark early days and move toward the success I have achieved.

I have realized every dream I had for myself when I first set foot in this country, and now I am thrilled to be able to assist you on your journey toward that same realization. To that end it is my great honor to announce the Million Dollar Success Institute, a thirteen-part online course designed to make the lessons you have learned in the pages of this book a reality in your life. Enrollees will experience a series of audio, video, PDF lessons, exercises and world-class coaching bonanza that will transform their entrepreneurial lives and drive them toward remarkable new levels of success. Should you decide to enroll, the course will offer high-powered tools that will help you break out of your comfort zone and begin living and thinking like a New American Millionaire. If networking is your goal, you will be sure to enjoy the members-only forum designed to spark interaction between hundreds of aspiring business owners with brilliant ideas.

The true beauty of the Million Dollar Success Institute is that it is action made into reality. It enhances everything you have learned in these pages; it places you in a virtual environment that allows you to *experience* the New American Millionaire way. You will find the online course exciting, enthralling, and packed with the wisdom, skills, and insights from some of this country's most successful entrepreneurs. As a bonus the program allows you access to the members area where you will find remarkable networking opportunities. Members will meet hundreds of people with a similar entrepreneurial spirit.

In this way we have recreated the kind of innovative and collaborative atmosphere that makes Silicon Valley the greatest place in the world to launch a technology business. You and your fellow members are likely to form bonds that will improve your businesses' scopes and capabilities and extend your reaches and potentials as entrepreneurs.

I leave you with this final piece of wisdom: nothing can be achieved until you act. You have your dream. You have your plan. You now know the traits that make an entrepreneur a millionaire in this modern marketplace. You have learned the steps to make those traits part of your reality. Now get out and make it happen. You can do this! Your future as a New American Millionaire begins now.

Acknowledgements

THIS BOOK REFLECTS THE contributions, insights, and toil of many persons. After all, if "it takes a village to raise a child," it also takes one to create a book of this caliber. First, there are many things I am thankful for. One of the greatest is the gift of foresighted parents who thought it wise to give me the opportunity to come to the United States at a very tender age to pursue my dream of a world-class education. Indeed this by itself was the beginning of my journey of proclivity toward writing this message for the benefit of myriad entrepreneurs. Therefore, I want to use this work to honor the memory of my father, Chief Gabriel Odiwe, whose inspiration to pursue the highest level of enlightenment in all endeavors is the guiding light of my life. Had he lived to see this day, Dad would have been very proud.

It is impossible to single out all the people who have contributed their time, energy, and expertise to the writing of this book. If I am remiss in mentioning some great individuals who gave their time to this project, I apologize from the bottom of my heart.

Frank Garon, I cannot begin to count all those precious hours of mentoring and encouragement you have brought to my life and work. I salute you not only because of your vast knowledge, but also for your simplicity of character and depth of kindness. I have learned enough wisdom from you to last a lifetime.

My dear friend, Kyle Fager, I am indebted to you for your tireless effort and those long hours you committed to helping in putting the manuscript in its present and readable form. You promised to do all that you can to bring this book to life and you certainly did.

Amber Ludwig, my marketing and web site expert, you are the best in the business. Your gentle nature combined with your undivided presence and attention to even the smallest detail should be made the standard for all professionals. Your spirit is beautiful.

Stefanie Hartman, my marketing strategist and business trend expert, you are a mentor to all mentors. Although I pride myself in being a business and marketing expert in my own right, I pale in comparison to your field experience in all its effectiveness. I honor you.

Mary Babic, for securing all the permissions needed. Alicia and Lorette Lyttle, I recognize you both for your friendship and online marketing training expertise. You are the most prolific connectors that I know. Cydney O'Sullivan, my Australian colleague and good friend. Thank you for the introductions to some of the most wonderful New American Millionaires. Jacqueline Lucien, your wonderful friendship and sagacious advice during the making of this project has guided me through the roughest of times. Our friendship means the world to me.

Preparation for a given outcome when in conjunction with opportunity inadvertently fosters success. Although my life is rated as a continuous journey toward success (and even more success as my previous goals are realized), some great teachers past and present, living or departed deserve mention as influential to my journey of becoming an expert through their books, seminars, and coaching programs.

Napoleon Hill – the original "success" author - for the dynamic teachings in his books. Failure is never an option for those who follow his techniques persistently. Dale Carnegie, Dr. Wayne Dyer, Stephen Covey, Brian Tracy, George Clason, Robin Sharma, T. Harv Eker, Jack Canfield, Mark Victor Hansen, Anthony Robins, Brendon Burchard, Michael Gerber, David Bach, Jim Rohn, Rick Frishman, David Hancock, Norman Vincent Peale, Og Mandino, Les Brown, John Assaraf, David

Schwartz, Robert Kiyosaki, Zig Ziglar, Wallace Wattles, Joel Osteen, Jay Abraham, Dan Kennedy, John Maxwell, Thomas Stanley, Joe Vitale, James Allen, Bob Proctor, Peter B. Kyne, Robert Cialdini, Susan Jeffers, Roger Dawson, Keith Ferrazzi, and Tim Ferriss—I owe you all a ton of gratitude for your enormous brilliance and the willingness to share with the world.

All my family, thank you for your encouragement, love, and support during the slow hours of writing this book. Thanks for understanding my mission and commission. The same goes to my life-long friends from academia and elsewhere, Dr. Derek Smith, Dr. Dan Kutz, Dr. Inno Ekeh, Dr. (Prof.) Christian Okeke, Sir Humphrey Okeke, and the rest of the gang. I salute you all.

The people who made themselves available for interviews or gave permission to reprint their thoughts and whose anecdotes and stories grace every section of this book, you are truly gracious: Jerry Yang, Vinod Khosla, Ric Fulop, Saeed Amidi, Dr. Naren Gupta, Henry Wong, Arjun Malhotra, Gabriel Nossovitch, David Yahid, Rajan Raghavan, Gershon Mader, and Massoud Kermani.

The following experts in their various fields have in recent years shared their precious marketing ideas, training/coaching, and wisdom that has helped me tremendously in breaking into the expert industry: Yanik Silver, Frank Garon, Eben Pagan, Jeff Walker, Frank Kern, Mike Koenigs, Brendon Burchard, Wendy Lipton-Dibner, Tom Antion, Dov Baron, Jill Lublin, Debbie Ford, Jeff Johnson, Rich Schefren, Alicia Lyttle, Lorette Lyttle, Armand Morin, John Carlton, Jay Conrad Levinson. I give my heartfelt thanks to all of you.

Finally, to all my readers, my current and future students in my mastery program, *The Million Dollar Success Institute,* and all those in-the trenches—entrepreneurs worldwide making it happen for themselves and their families—I am blessed and honored to be part of your community. Yours are exceptionally brilliant minds that turn "sand to gold." Truly you are all the best and brightest, and I thank you all.

About the Author

 **DR. KEN ODIWÉ** is the founder and CEO of Waterstone Management, a boutique consulting firm helping entrepreneurs and companies reach their peak performance. He is also the founder of the Million Dollar Success Institute. Dr. Ken is on a mission to share the secrets of *The New American Millionaires* with as many people as possible, so that they can experience the transformation that comes with increased wealth.

A voracious researcher, nurturing guide, teacher and success coach he knows what it takes to achieve your millionaire dreams in the 21st century. A New American Millionaire himself, his client base includes some of the fastest growing companies and associations in America as well as hundreds of executives and burgeoning entrepreneurs around the globe. He has used his training and coaching platforms to develop hundreds of success stories from his myriad clientele.

Dr. Ken has made it his lifelong calling to reach and assist entrepreneurs to advance from startup to controlling multi-million dollar businesses. He is one of the nation's leading and most sought after authorities on millionaire success principles.

Now you have the opportunity to learn from him as your personal mentor. This book is just the beginning of your personal journey of discovery and your game plan for success. Dr. Ken is in your corner, so you're not alone.

———

Discover more about Dr. Ken and claim your valuable Free Gifts at www.milliondollarsuccessinstitute.com